Cram101 Textbook Outlines to accompany:

Learning & Behavior

Chance, 5th Edition

An Academic Internet Publishers (AIPI) publication (c) 2007.

You have a discounted membership at www.Cram101.com with this book.

Get all of the practice tests for the chapters of this textbook, and access in-depth reference material for writing essays and papers. Here is an example from a Cram101 Biology text:

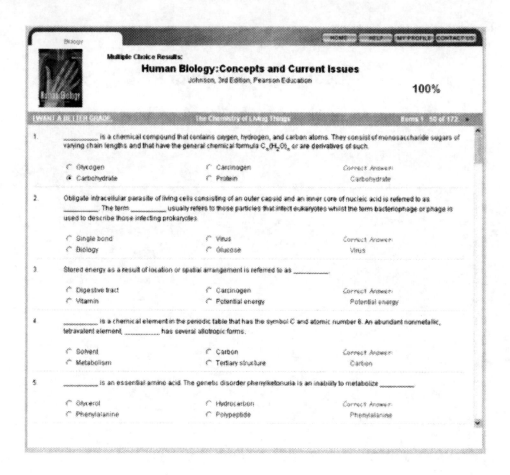

When you need problem solving help with math, stats, and other disciplines, www.Cram101.com will walk through the formulas and solutions step by step.

With Cram101.com online, you also have access to extensive reference material.

You will nail those essays and papers. Here is an example from a Cram101 Biology text:

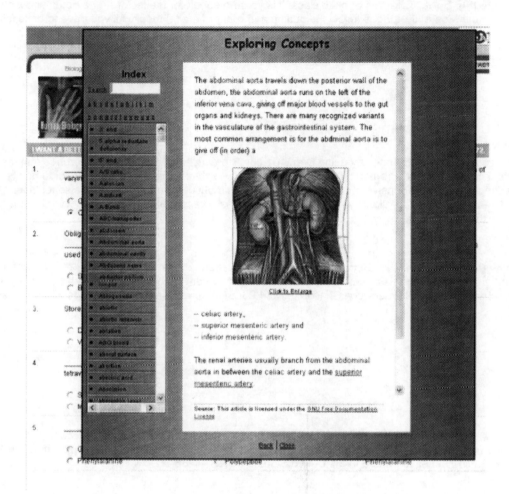

Visit **www.Cram101.com**, click Sign Up at the top of the screen, and enter DK73DW in the promo code box on the registration screen. Access to www.Cram101.com is normally $9.95, but because you have purchased this book, your access fee is only $4.95. Sign up and stop highlighting textbooks forever.

Learning System

Cram101 Textbook Outlines is a learning system. The notes in this book are the highlights of your textbook, you will never have to highlight a book again.

How to use this book. Take this book to class, it is your notebook for the lecture. The notes and highlights on the left hand side of the pages follow the outline and order of the textbook. All you have to do is follow along while your intructor presents the lecture. Circle the items emphasized in class and add other important information on the right side. With Cram101 Textbook Outlines you'll spend less time writing and more time listening. Learning becomes more efficient.

Cram101.com Online

Increase your studying efficiency by using Cram101.com's practice tests and online reference material. It is the perfect complement to Cram101 Textbook Outlines. Use self-teaching matching tests or simulate in-class testing with comprehensive multiple choice tests, or simply use Cram's true and false tests for quick review. Cram101.com even allows you to enter your in-class notes for an integrated studying format combining the textbook notes with your class notes.

Visit **www.Cram101.com**, click Sign Up at the top of the screen, and enter **DK73DW3528** in the promo code box on the registration screen. Access to www.Cram101.com is normally $9.95, but because you have purchased this book, your access fee is only $4.95. Sign up and stop highlighting textbooks forever.

Learning & Behavior
Chance, 5th

CONTENTS

Species	Species refers to a reproductively isolated breeding population.
Origin of Species	The Origin of Species by Charles Darwin makes the argument that groups of organisms gradually evolve through the process of natural selection. Characteristics that favor survival and reproduction are passed on to the next generation, those that do not, are gradually lost.
Natural selection	Natural selection is a process by which biological populations are altered over time, as a result of the propagation of heritable traits that affect the capacity of individual organisms to survive and reproduce.
Darwin	Darwin achieved lasting fame as originator of the theory of evolution through natural selection. His book Expression of Emotions in Man and Animals is generally considered the first text on comparative psychology.
Learning	Learning is a relatively permanent change in behavior that results from experience. Thus, to attribute a behavioral change to learning, the change must be relatively permanent and must result from experience.
Population	Population refers to all members of a well-defined group of organisms, events, or things.
Reflection	Reflection is the process of rephrasing or repeating thoughts and feelings expressed, making the person more aware of what they are saying or thinking.
Evolution	Commonly used to refer to gradual change, evolution is the change in the frequency of alleles within a population from one generation to the next. This change may be caused by different mechanisms, including natural selection, genetic drift, or changes in population (gene flow).
Selective breeding	Selective breeding refers to the mating of those members of a strain of animals or plants that manifest a particular characteristic, which may or may not be done deliberately, to affect the genetic makeup of future generations of that strain.
Direct observation	Direct observation refers to assessing behavior through direct surveillance.
Mendel	Mendel is often called the "father of genetics" for his study of the inheritance of traits in pea plants. Mendel showed that there was particulate inheritance of traits according to his laws of inheritance.
Gene	A gene is an ultramicroscopic area of the chromosome. It is the smallest physical unit of the DNA molecule that carries a piece of hereditary information.
Analogy	An analogy is a comparison between two different things, in order to highlight some form of similarity. Analogy is the cognitive process of transferring information from a particular subject to another particular subject.
Metaphor	A metaphor is a rhetorical trope where a comparison is made between two seemingly unrelated subjects
Trait	An enduring personality characteristic that tends to lead to certain behaviors is called a trait. The term trait also means a genetically inherited feature of an organism.
Adaptation	Adaptation is a lowering of sensitivity to a stimulus following prolonged exposure to that stimulus. Behavioral adaptations are special ways a particular organism behaves to survive in its natural habitat.
Mutation	Mutation is a permanent, sometimes transmissible (if the change is to a germ cell) change to the genetic material (usually DNA or RNA) of a cell. They can be caused by copying errors in the genetic material during cell division and by exposure to radiation, chemicals, or viruses, or can occur deliberately under cellular control during the processes such as meiosis or hypermutation.
Fixed action pattern	A behavior that occurs in essentially identical fashion among most members of a species, that is elicited by a specific environmental stimulus, and is typically more complex than a reflex, is a fixed

	action pattern.
Adaptive behavior	An adaptive behavior increases the probability of the individual or organism to survive or exist within its environment.
Innate	Innate behavior is not learned or influenced by the environment, rather, it is present or predisposed at birth.
Reflex	A simple, involuntary response to a stimulus is referred to as reflex. Reflex actions originate at the spinal cord rather than the brain.
Stages	Stages represent relatively discrete periods of time in which functioning is qualitatively different from functioning at other periods.
Lungs	The lungs are the essential organs of respiration. Its principal function is to transport oxygen from the atmosphere into the bloodstream, and excrete carbon dioxide from the bloodstream into the atmosphere.
Iris	The iris is the most visible part of the eye. The iris is an annulus (or flattened ring) consisting of pigmented fibrovascular tissue known as a stroma. The stroma connects a sphincter muscle, which contracts the pupil, and a set of dialator muscles which open it.
Rooting reflex	The rooting reflex is a newborn's built-in reaction that occurs when the infant's cheek is stroked or the side of the mouth is touched. In response, the infant turns its head toward the side that was touched in an apparent effort to find something to suck.
Sucking reflex	The sucking reflex is a newborn's built-in reaction of automatically sucking an object placed in its mouth. The sucking reflex enables the infant to get nourishment before it has associated a nipple with food.
Central nervous system	The vertebrate central nervous system consists of the brain and spinal cord.
Alcoholic	An alcoholic is dependent on alcohol as characterized by craving, loss of control, physical dependence and withdrawal symptoms, and tolerance.
Seizure	A seizure is a temporary alteration in brain function expressed as a changed mental state, tonic or clonic movements and various other symptoms. They are due to temporary abnormal electrical activity of a group of brain cells.
Binge drinking	Binge drinking refers to consuming 5 or more drinks in a short time or drinking alchohol for the sole purpose of intoxication.
Sensitization	Sensitization is a process whereby an organism is made more responsive to certain aspects of its environment. For example, increases in the effects of a drug as a result of repeated administration. Also known as reverse tolerance.
Drug addiction	Drug addiction, or substance dependence is the compulsive use of drugs, to the point where the user has no effective choice but to continue use.
Addictive drugs	Addictive drugs produce a biological or psychological dependence in the user; withdrawal from them leads to a craving for the drug that in some cases can be nearly irresistible.
Morphine	Morphine, the principal active agent in opium, is a powerful opioid analgesic drug. According to recent research, it may also be produced naturally by the human brain. Morphine is usually highly addictive, and tolerance and physical and psychological dependence develop quickly.
Galvanic skin response	Galvanic skin response is a method of measuring the electrical resistance of the skin and interpreting it as an image of activity in certain parts of the body.
Stimulus	A change in an environmental condition that elicits a response is a stimulus.

Habituation	In habituation there is a progressive reduction in the response probability with continued repetition of a stimulus.
Brain	The brain controls and coordinates most movement, behavior and homeostatic body functions such as heartbeat, blood pressure, fluid balance and body temperature. Functions of the brain are responsible for cognition, emotion, memory, motor learning and other sorts of learning. The brain is primarily made up of two types of cells: glia and neurons.
Fetus	A fetus develops from the end of the 8th week of pregnancy (when the major structures have formed), until birth.
Loudness	Loudness is the quality of a sound that is the primary psychological correlate of physical intensity. Loudness is often approximated by a power function with an exponent of 0.6 when plotted vs. sound pressure or 0.3 when plotted vs. sound intensity.
Prenatal	Prenatal period refers to the time from conception to birth.
Variable	A variable refers to a measurable factor, characteristic, or attribute of an individual or a system.
Variability	Statistically, variability refers to how much the scores in a distribution spread out, away from the mean.
Gland	A gland is an organ in an animal's body that synthesizes a substance for release such as hormones, often into the bloodstream or into cavities inside the body or its outer surface.
Instinct	Instinct is the word used to describe inherent dispositions towards particular actions. They are generally an inherited pattern of responses or reactions to certain kinds of situations.
Genitals	Genitals refers to the internal and external reproductive organs.
Pheromone	A pheromone is any chemical produced by a living organism that transmits a message to other members of the same species. There are alarm pheromones, food trail pheromones, sex pheromones, and many others. Their use among insects has been particularly well documented, although many vertebrates also communicate using pheromones. Their use by humans is controversial.
Estrus	The estrus cycle refers to the recurring physiologic changes that are induced by reproductive hormones in most mammalian placental females (humans and great apes are the only mammals who undergo a menstrual cycle instead).
Skinner	Skinner conducted research on shaping behavior through positive and negative reinforcement, and demonstrated operant conditioning, a technique which he developed in contrast with classical conditioning.
McDougall	McDougall was important in the development of the theory of instinct and of social psychology. Opposing behaviorism, he argued that behavior was generally goal-oriented and purposive, an approach he called hormic psychology; in the theory of motivation he held that individuals are motivated by a significant number of inherited instincts so they might not always understand their own goals.
Nurture	Nurture refers to the environmental influences on behavior due to nutrition, culture, socioeconomic status, and learning.
Kibbutz	Kibbutz is an Israeli farming community in which children are reared in group settings.
Sigmund Freud	Sigmund Freud was the founder of the psychoanalytic school, based on his theory that unconscious motives control much behavior, that particular kinds of unconscious thoughts and memories are the source of neurosis, and that neurosis could be treated through bringing these unconscious thoughts and memories to consciousness in psychoanalytic treatment.
Incest	Incest refers to sexual relations between close relatives, most often between daughter and father or between brother and sister.
Genetics	Genetics is the science of genes, heredity, and the variation of organisms.

Introversion	A personality trait characterized by intense imagination and a tendency to inhibit impulses is called introversion.
Anxiety	Anxiety is a complex combination of the feeling of fear, apprehension and worry often accompanied by physical sensations such as palpitations, chest pain and/or shortness of breath.
Plasticity	The capacity for modification and change is referred to as plasticity.
Heredity	Heredity is the transfer of characteristics from parent to offspring through their genes.
Addiction	Addiction is an uncontrollable compulsion to repeat a behavior regardless of its consequences. Many drugs or behaviors can precipitate a pattern of conditions recognized as addiction, which include a craving for more of the drug or behavior, increased physiological tolerance to exposure, and withdrawal symptoms in the absence of the stimulus.
Habit	A habit is a response that has become completely separated from its eliciting stimulus. Early learning theorists used the term to describe S-R associations, however not all S-R associations become a habit, rather many are extinguished after reinforcement is withdrawn.
Quantitative	A quantitative property is one that exists in a range of magnitudes, and can therefore be measured. Measurements of any particular quantitative property are expressed as as a specific quantity, referred to as a unit, multiplied by a number.
Fraternal twins	Fraternal twins usually occur when two fertilized eggs are implanted in the uterine wall at the same time. The two eggs form two zygotes, and these twins are therefore also known as dizygotic. Dizygotic twins are no more similar genetically than any siblings.
Identical twins	Identical twins occur when a single egg is fertilized to form one zygote (monozygotic) but the zygote then divides into two separate embryos. The two embryos develop into foetuses sharing the same womb. Monozygotic twins are genetically identical unless there has been a mutation in development, and they are almost always the same gender.
Homosexual	Homosexual refers to a sexual orientation characterized by aesthetic attraction, romantic love, and sexual desire exclusively for members of the same sex or gender identity.
Lesbian	A lesbian is a homosexual woman. They are women who are sexually and romantically attracted to other women.
Anxiety disorder	Anxiety disorder is a blanket term covering several different forms of abnormal anxiety, fear, phobia and nervous condition, that come on suddenly and prevent pursuing normal daily routines.
Schizophrenia	Schizophrenia is characterized by persistent defects in the perception or expression of reality. A person suffering from untreated schizophrenia typically demonstrates grossly disorganized thinking, and may also experience delusions or auditory hallucinations
Mental illness	Mental illness is the term formerly used to mean psychological disorder but less preferred because it implies that the causes of the disorder can be found in a medical disease process.
Bandura	Bandura is best known for his work on social learning theory or Social Cognitivism. His famous Bobo doll experiment illustrated that people learn from observing others.
Extinction	In operant extinction, if no reinforcement is delivered after the response, gradually the behavior will no longer occur in the presence of the stimulus. The process is more rapid following continuous reinforcement rather than after partial reinforcement. In Classical Conditioning, repeated presentations of the CS without being followed by the US results in the extinction of the CS.
Early adulthood	The developmental period beginning in the late teens or early twenties and lasting into the thirties is called early adulthood; characterized by an increasing self-awareness.
Defense mechanism	A Defense mechanism is a set of unconscious ways to protect one's personality from unpleasant thoughts and realities which may otherwise cause anxiety. The notion is an integral part of the psychoanalytic

theory.

Immune system	The most important function of the human immune system occurs at the cellular level of the blood and tissues. The lymphatic and blood circulation systems are highways for specialized white blood cells. These cells include B cells, T cells, natural killer cells, and macrophages. All function with the primary objective of recognizing, attacking and destroying bacteria, viruses, cancer cells, and all substances seen as foreign.
Affect	A subjective feeling or emotional tone often accompanied by bodily expressions noticeable to others is called affect.
E. O. Wilson	E. O. Wilson is an entomologist and biologist known for his work on ecology, evolution, and sociobiology. Sociobiology suggests that animal, and by extension human, behavior can be studied using an evolutionary framework.
Nature-nurture	Nature-nurture is a shorthand expression for debates about the relative importance of an individual's "nature" versus personal experiences ("nurture") in determining or causing physical and behavioral traits.
Insanity	A legal status indicating that a person cannot be held responsible for his or her actions because of mental illness is called insanity.
Harlow	Harlow and his famous wire and cloth surrogate mother monkey studies demonstrated that the need for affection created a stronger bond between mother and infant than did physical needs. He also found that the more discrimination problems the monkeys solved, the better they became at solving them.
Nervous breakdown	Nervous breakdown is often used by laymen to describe a sudden and acute attack of mental illness—for instance, clinical depression or anxiety disorder—in a previously outwardly healthy person. Breakdowns are the result of chronic and unrelenting nervous strain, and not a sign of weakness.
Pavlov	Pavlov first described the phenomenon now known as classical conditioning in experiments with dogs.
Abnormal behavior	An action, thought, or feeling that is harmful to the person or to others is called abnormal behavior.
Maladjustment	Maladjustment is the condition of being unable to adapt properly to your environment with resulting emotional instability.
Positive feedback	When a change in a variable occurs in a system, the system responds. In the case of positive feedback the response of the system is to cause that variable to increase in the same direction.
Socioeconomic	Socioeconomic pertains to the study of the social and economic impacts of any product or service offering, market intervention or other activity on an economy as a whole and on the companies, organization and individuals who are its main economic actors.
Evolutionary theory	Evolutionary theory is concerned with heritable variability rather than behavioral variations. Natural selection requirements: (1) natural variability within a species must exist, (2) only some individual differences are heritable, and (3) natural selection only takes place when there is an interaction between the inborn attributes of organisms and the environment in which they live.

10

Go to **Cram101.com** for the Practice Tests for this Chapter.

Learning	Learning is a relatively permanent change in behavior that results from experience. Thus, to attribute a behavioral change to learning, the change must be relatively permanent and must result from experience.
Experimental psychology	Experimental psychology is an approach to psychology that treats it as one of the natural sciences, and therefore assumes that it is susceptible to the experimental method.
Acquisition	Acquisition is the process of adapting to the environment, learning or becoming conditioned. In classical conditoning terms, it is the initial learning of the stimulus response link, which involves a neutral stimulus being associated with a unconditioned stimulus and becoming a conditioned stimulus.
Scientific method	Psychologists gather data in order to describe, understand, predict, and control behavior. Scientific method refers to an approach that can be used to discover accurate information. It includes these steps: understand the problem, collect data, draw conclusions, and revise research conclusions.
Cognitive structure	According to Piaget, the number of schemata available to an organism at any given time constitutes that organism's cognitive structure. How the organism interacts with its environment depends on the current cognitive structure available. As the cognitive structure develops, new assimilations can occur.
Society	The social sciences use the term society to mean a group of people that form a semi-closed (or semi-open) social system, in which most interactions are with other individuals belonging to the group.
Innate	Innate behavior is not learned or influenced by the environment, rather, it is present or predisposed at birth.
Nervous system	The body's electrochemical communication circuitry, made up of billions of neurons is a nervous system.
Brain	The brain controls and coordinates most movement, behavior and homeostatic body functions such as heartbeat, blood pressure, fluid balance and body temperature. Functions of the brain are responsible for cognition, emotion, memory, motor learning and other sorts of learning. The brain is primarily made up of two types of cells: glia and neurons.
Physiology	The study of the functions and activities of living cells, tissues, and organs and of the physical and chemical phenomena involved is referred to as physiology.
Operational definition	An operational definition is the definition of a concept or action in terms of the observable and repeatable process, procedures, and appartaus that illustrates the concept or action.
Gland	A gland is an organ in an animal's body that synthesizes a substance for release such as hormones, often into the bloodstream or into cavities inside the body or its outer surface.
Emotion	An emotion is a mental states that arise spontaneously, rather than through conscious effort. They are often accompanied by physiological changes.
Verbal Behavior	Verbal Behavior is a book written by B.F. Skinner in which the author presents his ideas on language. For Skinner, speech, along with other forms of communication, was simply a behavior. Skinner argued that each act of speech is an inevitable consequence of the speaker's current environment and his behavioral and sensory history.
Stimulus	A change in an environmental condition that elicits a response is a stimulus.
Maturation	The orderly unfolding of traits, as regulated by the genetic code is called maturation.
Tolman	Tolman coined the term "cognitive map", which was an internal perceptual representation of external environmental features and landmarks. He is virtually the only behaviorist who found the Stimulus-Response theory unacceptable, because reinforcement was not necessary for

	learning to occur. He felt behavior was holistic, purposive, and cognitive.
Reflection	Reflection is the process of rephrasing or repeating thoughts and feelings expressed, making the person more aware of what they are saying or thinking.
Hull	Hull is best known for the Drive Reduction Theory which postulated that behavior occurs in response to primary drives such as hunger, thirst, sexual interest, etc. When the goal of the drive is attained the drive is reduced. This reduction of drive serves as a reinforcer for learning.
Latency	In child development, latency refers to a phase of psychosexual development characterized by repression of sexual impulses. In learning theory, latency is the delay between stimulus (S) and response (R), which according to Hull depends on the strength of the association.
Decoding	Process of phonetic analysis by which a printed word is converted to spoken form before retrieval from long-term memory is called decoding.
Skinner	Skinner conducted research on shaping behavior through positive and negative reinforcement, and demonstrated operant conditioning, a technique which he developed in contrast with classical conditioning.
Response rate	The response rate is usually calculated by dividing the total number of responses by the time available for the response.
Automaticity	The ability to process information with little or no effort is referred to as automaticity.
Research design	A research design tests a hypothesis. The basic typess are: descriptive, correlational, and experimental.
Anecdotal evidence	Anecdotal evidence is unreliable evidence based on personal experience that has not been empirically tested, and which is often used in an argument as if it had been scientifically or statistically proven. The person using anecdotal evidence may or may not be aware of the fact that, by doing so, they are generalizing.
Wisdom	Wisdom is the ability to make correct judgments and decisions. It is an intangible quality gained through experience. Whether or not something is wise is determined in a pragmatic sense by its popularity, how long it has been around, and its ability to predict against future events.
Variable	A variable refers to a measurable factor, characteristic, or attribute of an individual or a system.
Case study	A carefully drawn biography that may be obtained through interviews, questionnaires, and psychological tests is called a case study.
Descriptive study	Any study in which the researcher describes the behavior of an individual or set of individuals without systematically investigating relationships between specific variables is a descriptive study.
Questionnaire	A self-report method of data collection or clinical assessment method in which the individual being studied checks off items on a printed list, answers multiple-choice questions, or writes out answers to essay questions aimed at producing a selfdescription is called questionnaire.
Phobia	A persistent, irrational fear of an object, situation, or activity that the person feels compelled to avoid is referred to as a phobia.
Independent variable	A condition in a scientific study that is manipulated (assigned different values by a researcher) so that the effects of the manipulation may be observed is called an independent variable.

Dependent variable	A measure of an assumed effect of an independent variable is called the dependent variable.
Between-subjects design	Between-subjects design is an experimental design in which comparisons are made between one group and another. Participants in a given group do not receive the same level of the independent variable or treatment as those in another group.
Experimental group	Experimental group refers to any group receiving a treatment effect in an experiment.
Control group	A group that does not receive the treatment effect in an experiment is referred to as the control group or sometimes as the comparison group.
Hartup	According to Hartup, the single best childhood predictor of adult adaptation is not school grades, and not classroom behavior, but rather, the adequacy with which the child gets along with other children.
Random assignment	Assignment of participants to experimental and control groups by chance is called random assignment. Random assigment reduces the likelihood that the results are due to preexisiting systematic differences between the groups.
Matched sampling	Matched sampling is a procedure for reducing extraneous differences among subjects in between-subjects experiments by matching those in the experimental and control groups on specified characteristics, such as age, sex, and weight.
Socioeconomic	Socioeconomic pertains to the study of the social and economic impacts of any product or service offering, market intervention or other activity on an economy as a whole and on the companies, organization and individuals who are its main economic actors.
Conditioning	Conditioning describes the process by which behaviors can be learned or modified through interaction with the environment.
Baseline period	In a within-subject experiment, a period of observation during which no attempt is made to modify the behavior under study is referred to as the baseline period.
Baseline	Measure of a particular behavior or process taken before the introduction of the independent variable or treatment is called the baseline.
Aba reversal design	An ABA reversal design is a type of within subject experiment in which behavior is observed before and after an experimental manipulation. The original condition is restored, sometimes followed again by the experimental condition.
Statistics	Statistics is a type of data analysis which practice includes the planning, summarizing, and interpreting of observations of a system possibly followed by predicting or forecasting of future events based on a mathematical model of the system being observed.
Field experiment	A field experiment applies the scientific method to experimentally examine an intervention in the real world rather than in the laboratory. Field experiments generally randomize subjects into treatment and control groups and compare outcomes between these groups.
Identical twins	Identical twins occur when a single egg is fertilized to form one zygote (monozygotic) but the zygote then divides into two separate embryos. The two embryos develop into foetuses sharing the same womb. Monozygotic twins are genetically identical unless there has been a mutation in development, and they are almost always the same gender.
Variability	Statistically, variability refers to how much the scores in a distribution spread out, away from the mean.
Species	Species refers to a reproductively isolated breeding population.
Affect	A subjective feeling or emotional tone often accompanied by bodily expressions noticeable to

others is called affect.

Mental retardation	Mental retardation refers to having significantly below-average intellectual functioning and limitations in at least two areas of adaptive functioning. Many categorize retardation as mild, moderate, severe, or profound.
Hyperactivity	Hyperactivity can be described as a state in which a individual is abnormally easily excitable and exuberant. Strong emotional reactions and a very short span of attention is also typical for the individual.
Depression	In everyday language depression refers to any downturn in mood, which may be relatively transitory and perhaps due to something trivial. This is differentiated from Clinical depression which is marked by symptoms that last two weeks or more and are so severe that they interfere with daily living.
Dyslexia	Dyslexia is a neurological disorder with biochemical and genetic markers. In its most common and apparent form, it is a disability in which a person's reading and/or writing ability is significantly lower than that which would be predicted by his or her general level of intelligence.
Syndrome	The term syndrome is the association of several clinically recognizable features, signs, symptoms, phenomena or characteristics which often occur together, so that the presence of one feature indicates the presence of the others.
Autism	Autism is a neurodevelopmental disorder that manifests itself in markedly abnormal social interaction, communication ability, patterns of interests, and patterns of behavior.
Motives	Needs or desires that energize and direct behavior toward a goal are motives.
Basic research	Basic research has as its primary objective the advancement of knowledge and the theoretical understanding of the relations among variables . It is exploratory and often driven by the researcher's curiosity, interest or hunch.
Reinforcement	In operant conditioning, reinforcement is any change in an environment that (a) occurs after the behavior, (b) seems to make that behavior re-occur more often in the future and (c) that reoccurence of behavior must be the result of the change.
Research method	The scope of the research method is to produce some new knowledge. This, in principle, can take three main forms: Exploratory research; Constructive research; and Empirical research.
Scientific research	Research that is objective, systematic, and testable is called scientific research.
Addiction	Addiction is an uncontrollable compulsion to repeat a behavior regardless of its consequences. Many drugs or behaviors can precipitate a pattern of conditions recognized as addiction, which include a craving for more of the drug or behavior, increased physiological tolerance to exposure, and withdrawal symptoms in the absence of the stimulus.
Cocaine	Cocaine is a crystalline tropane alkaloid that is obtained from the leaves of the coca plant. It is a stimulant of the central nervous system and an appetite suppressant, creating what has been described as a euphoric sense of happiness and increased energy.

Higher-order conditioning	In classical conditioning a neutral stimulus comes to elicit a condtioned response(CR) through repeated pairings of the neutral stimulus with a natural or unconditioned stimulus that results in that response. The nuetral stimulus is now called a conditioned stimulus(CS). That CS can also be paired with another nuetral stimulus to produce a higher-order conditioning; a chain of CS-CR relationships.
Pavlovian conditioning	Pavlovian conditioning, synonymous with classical conditioning is a type of learning found in animals, caused by the association (or pairing) of two stimuli or what Ivan Pavlov described as the learning of conditional behavior, therefore called conditioning.
Conditional response	A conditional response is elicited by a conditional stimulus in a conditional reflex.
Conditioning	Conditioning describes the process by which behaviors can be learned or modified through interaction with the environment.
Extinction	In operant extinction, if no reinforcement is delivered after the response, gradually the behavior will no longer occur in the presence of the stimulus. The process is more rapid following continuous reinforcement rather than after partial reinforcement. In Classical Conditioning, repeated presentations of the CS without being followed by the US results in the extinction of the CS.
Learning	Learning is a relatively permanent change in behavior that results from experience. Thus, to attribute a behavioral change to learning, the change must be relatively permanent and must result from experience.
Variable	A variable refers to a measurable factor, characteristic, or attribute of an individual or a system.
Theories	Theories are logically self-consistent models or frameworks describing the behavior of a certain natural or social phenomenon. They are broad explanations and predictions concerning phenomena of interest.
Pavlov	Pavlov first described the phenomenon now known as classical conditioning in experiments with dogs.
Gland	A gland is an organ in an animal's body that synthesizes a substance for release such as hormones, often into the bloodstream or into cavities inside the body or its outer surface.
Reflex	A simple, involuntary response to a stimulus is referred to as reflex. Reflex actions originate at the spinal cord rather than the brain.
Origin of Species	The Origin of Species by Charles Darwin makes the argument that groups of organisms gradually evolve through the process of natural selection. Characteristics that favor survival and reproduction are passed on to the next generation, those that do not, are gradually lost.
Darwin	Darwin achieved lasting fame as originator of the theory of evolution through natural selection. His book Expression of Emotions in Man and Animals is generally considered the first text on comparative psychology.
Sensation	Sensation is the first stage in the chain of biochemical and neurologic events that begins with the impinging of a stimulus upon the receptor cells of a sensory organ, which then leads to perception, the mental state that is reflected in statements like "I see a uniformly blue wall."
Species	Species refers to a reproductively isolated breeding population.
Yerkes	Yerkes worked in the field of comparative psychology. He is best known for studying the intelligence and social behavior of gorillas and chimpanzees. Joining with John D. Dodson, he developed the Yerkes-Dodson law relating arousal to performance.

Go to **Cram101.com** for the Practice Tests for this Chapter.

Thorndike	Thorndike worked in animal behavior and the learning process leading to the theory of connectionism. Among his most famous contributions were his research on cats escaping from puzzle boxes, and his formulation of the Law of Effect.
Conditional stimulus	A conditional stimulus in a conditional reflex elicits a conditional response.
Stimulus	A change in an environmental condition that elicits a response is a stimulus.
Neutral stimulus	A stimulus prior to conditioning that does not naturally result in the response of interest is called a neutral stimulus.
Gene	A gene is an ultramicroscopic area of the chromosome. It is the smallest physical unit of the DNA molecule that carries a piece of hereditary information.
Hormone	A hormone is a chemical messenger from one cell (or group of cells) to another. The best known are those produced by endocrine glands, but they are produced by nearly every organ system. The function of hormones is to serve as a signal to the target cells; the action of the hormone is determined by the pattern of secretion and the signal transduction of the receiving tissue.
Graham	Graham has conducted a number of studies that reveal stronger socioeconomic-status influences rather than ethnic influences in achievement.
Pheromone	A pheromone is any chemical produced by a living organism that transmits a message to other members of the same species. There are alarm pheromones, food trail pheromones, sex pheromones, and many others. Their use among insects has been particularly well documented, although many vertebrates also communicate using pheromones. Their use by humans is controversial.
Conditional reflex	A reflex acquired through Pavlovian conditioning and consisting of a conditional stimulus and a conditional response is a conditional reflex.
Innate	Innate behavior is not learned or influenced by the environment, rather, it is present or predisposed at birth.
Respondent Conditioning	Respondent conditioning refers to behavior that is elicited involuntarily as a reaction to a stimulus. Respondent behavior is identical to classical conditioning UC to UR relationships.
Adaptation	Adaptation is a lowering of sensitivity to a stimulus following prolonged exposure to that stimulus. Behavioral adaptations are special ways a particular organism behaves to survive in its natural habitat.
Nonsense syllable	A nonsense syllable is a consonant-vowel-consonant combination that does not spell a word. It is an experimental methodology invented by Ebbinghaus to control for the meaningfulness of the material in studies of memory.
Latency	In child development, latency refers to a phase of psychosexual development characterized by repression of sexual impulses. In learning theory, latency is the delay between stimulus (S) and response (R), which according to Hull depends on the strength of the association.
Rescorla	Rescorla agreed with Pavlov that for learning to take place, the CS had to be a useful predictor of the US. But he disagreed on what made the CS a useful predictor. It was more complicated than the number of CS-US pairings. He maintained that it was the contingency between the CS and US.
Amplitude	Amplitude is a nonnegative scalar measure of a wave's magnitude of oscillation.
Sensitization	Sensitization is a process whereby an organism is made more responsive to certain aspects of its environment. For example, increases in the effects of a drug as a result of repeated administration. Also known as reverse tolerance.

Go to **Cram101.com** for the Practice Tests for this Chapter.

Control subjects	Control subjects are participants in an experiment who do not receive the treatment effect but for whom all other conditions are held comparable to those of experimental subjects.
Control group	A group that does not receive the treatment effect in an experiment is referred to as the control group or sometimes as the comparison group.
Pseudocondit-oning	Pseudoconditioning is the tendency of a neutral stimulus to elicit a conditioned response when presented after an unconditioned stimulus has elicited a reflex response. It is apparently due to sensitization.
Trace conditioning	A classical conditioning procedure in which the CS is presented and then removed before the US is presented is called trace conditioning.
Delayed conditioning	A classical conditioning procedure in which the CS is presented before the US and remains in place until the response occurs is called delayed conditioning.
Simultaneous conditioning	A classical conditioning procedure in which the CS and US are presented at the same time is referred to as simultaneous conditioning.
Backward conditioning	A classical conditioning procedure in which the unconditioned stimulus is presented before the conditioned stimulus is called backward conditioning. It is seldom effective.
Response rate	The response rate is usually calculated by dividing the total number of responses by the time available for the response.
Affect	A subjective feeling or emotional tone often accompanied by bodily expressions noticeable to others is called affect.
Compound stimulus	A compound stimulus refers to two or more stimuli presented simultaneously.
Tactile	Pertaining to the sense of touch is referred to as tactile.
Kamin	Kamin argues that blocking is caused by lack of learning. In the compound stimulus training, there is lack of surprise about the outcome because one of the members of the compound stimulus already predicts the outcome. There is no surprise effect, therefore no learning.
Acquisition	Acquisition is the process of adapting to the environment, learning or becoming conditioned. In classical conditoning terms, it is the initial learning of the stimulus response link, which involves a neutral stimulus being associated with a unconditioned stimulus and becoming a conditioned stimulus.
Receptor	A sensory receptor is a structure that recognizes a stimulus in the internal or external environment of an organism. In response to stimuli the sensory receptor initiates sensory transduction by creating graded potentials or action potentials in the same cell or in an adjacent one.
Latent inhibition	If after the habituation of a stimulus, it is later paired with a US the conditioning may be weak and unstable. This effect is called latent inhibition.
Overshadowing	Overshadowing refers to the failure of a stimulus that is part of a compound stimulus to become a CS.
Blocking	If the one of the two members of a compound stimulus fails to produce the CR due to an earlier conditioning of the other member of the compound stimulus, blocking has occurred.
Intertrial interval	The intertrial interval separates the trials of a discrete trial procedure.
Dementia	Dementia is progressive decline in cognitive function due to damage or disease in the brain beyond what might be expected from normal aging.

Stages	Stages represent relatively discrete periods of time in which functioning is qualitatively different from functioning at other periods.
Anxiety	Anxiety is a complex combination of the feeling of fear, apprehension and worry often accompanied by physical sensations such as palpitations, chest pain and/or shortness of breath.
Rate of learning	The rate of learning is the change in responding due to the presence of a stimulus, over time.
Hilgard	Hilgard made headlines as a pioneer in the scientific study of hypnosis. He and his wife, Josephine, established the Laboratory of Hypnosis Research at Stanford.
Spontaneous recovery	The recurrence of an extinguished response as a function of the passage of time is referred to as spontaneous recovery.
Construct	A generalized concept, such as anxiety or gravity, is a construct.
American Psychological Association	The American Psychological Association is a professional organization representing psychology in the US. The mission statement is to "advance psychology as a science and profession and as a means of promoting health, education , and human welfare".
William James	Functionalism as a psychology developed out of Pragmatism as a philosophy: To find the meaning of an idea, you have to look at its consequences. This led William James and his students towards an emphasis on cause and effect, prediction and control, and observation of environment and behavior, over the careful introspection of the Structuralists.
Brain	The brain controls and coordinates most movement, behavior and homeostatic body functions such as heartbeat, blood pressure, fluid balance and body temperature. Functions of the brain are responsible for cognition, emotion, memory, motor learning and other sorts of learning. The brain is primarily made up of two types of cells: glia and neurons.
Analogy	An analogy is a comparison between two different things, in order to highlight some form of similarity. Analogy is the cognitive process of transferring information from a particular subject to another particular subject.
Preparatory response theory	The preparatory response theory of Pavlovian conditioning proposes that the conditioned response prepares the organism for the occurrence of the unconditioned stimulus.
Addictive drugs	Addictive drugs produce a biological or psychological dependence in the user; withdrawal from them leads to a craving for the drug that in some cases can be nearly irresistible.
Morphine	Morphine, the principal active agent in opium, is a powerful opioid analgesic drug. According to recent research, it may also be produced naturally by the human brain. Morphine is usually highly addictive, and tolerance and physical and psychological dependence develop quickly.
Galvanic skin response	Galvanic skin response is a method of measuring the electrical resistance of the skin and interpreting it as an image of activity in certain parts of the body.
Drug tolerance	Drug tolerance occurs when a subject's reaction to a drug (such as a painkiller or intoxicant) decreases so that larger doses are required to achieve the same effect. In addicted patients, the resulting pattern of uncontrolled escalating doses may lead to drug overdose.
Heroin	Heroin is widely and illegally used as a powerful and addictive drug producing intense euphoria, which often disappears with increasing tolerance. Heroin is a semi-synthetic opioid. It is the 3,6-diacetyl derivative of morphine and is synthesised from it by acetylation.
Functional analysis	A systematic study of behavior in which one identifies the stimuli that trigger the behavior and the reinforcers that maintain it is a functional analysis. Relations between the two

become the cause-and-effect relationships in behavior and are the laws of a science. A synthesis of these various laws expressed in quantitative terms yields a comprehensive picture of the organism as a behaving system without postulating internal processes.

Physiology

The study of the functions and activities of living cells, tissues, and organs and of the physical and chemical phenomena involved is referred to as physiology.

Insomnia

Insomnia is a sleep disorder characterized by an inability to sleep and/or to remain asleep for a reasonable period during the night.

Paraphilia	Paraphilia is a sexual disorder in which sexual urges, fantasies, and behavior generally involve children, other nonconsenting partners, nonhuman objects, or the suffering and humiliation of oneself or one's partner .
Pavlovian conditioning	Pavlovian conditioning, synonymous with classical conditioning is a type of learning found in animals, caused by the association (or pairing) of two stimuli or what Ivan Pavlov described as the learning of conditional behavior, therefore called conditioning.
Pavlov	Pavlov first described the phenomenon now known as classical conditioning in experiments with dogs.
Human nature	Human nature is the fundamental nature and substance of humans, as well as the range of human behavior that is believed to be invariant over long periods of time and across very different cultural contexts.
Insight	Insight refers to a sudden awareness of the relationships among various elements that had previously appeared to be independent of one another.
Adaptation	Adaptation is a lowering of sensitivity to a stimulus following prolonged exposure to that stimulus. Behavioral adaptations are special ways a particular organism behaves to survive in its natural habitat.
Learning	Learning is a relatively permanent change in behavior that results from experience. Thus, to attribute a behavioral change to learning, the change must be relatively permanent and must result from experience.
Emotion	An emotion is a mental states that arise spontaneously, rather than through conscious effort. They are often accompanied by physiological changes.
Reasoning	Reasoning is the act of using reason to derive a conclusion from certain premises. There are two main methods to reach a conclusion,deductive reasoning and inductive reasoning.
Conditioned emotional response	Conditioned emotional response refers to an emotional response that has been linked to a previously non-emotional stimulus by classical conditioning.
Phobia	A persistent, irrational fear of an object, situation, or activity that the person feels compelled to avoid is referred to as a phobia.
Fear response	In the Mowrer-Miller theory, a response to a threatening or noxious situation that is covert but that is assumed to function as a stimulus to produce measurable physiological changes in the body and observable overt behavior is referred to as the fear response.
Stimulus	A change in an environmental condition that elicits a response is a stimulus.
Little Albert	The Little Albert experiment was an experiment showing empirical evidence of classical conditioning in children. The actual experiment with Little Albert on conditioned fear involved exposing the child to a loud sound while being presented with a white rat.
Countercondi-ioning	The process of eliminating a classically conditioned response by pairing the CS with an unconditioned stimulus for a response that is stronger than the conditioned response and that cannot occur at the same time as the CR is called counterconditioning.
Mary Cover Jones	Mary Cover Jones stands out as a pioneer of behavior therapy. Her study of unconditioning a fear of rabbits in a three-year-old named Peter is her most often cited work.
Infancy	The developmental period that extends from birth to 18 or 24 months is called infancy.
Anxiety	Anxiety is a complex combination of the feeling of fear, apprehension and worry often accompanied by physical sensations such as palpitations, chest pain and/or shortness of breath.

Conditioning	Conditioning describes the process by which behaviors can be learned or modified through interaction with the environment.
Systematic desensitization	Systematic desensitization refers to Wolpe's behavioral fear-reduction technique in which a hierarchy of fear-evoking stimuli are presented while the person remains relaxed. The fear-evoking stimuli thereby become associated with muscle relaxation.
Virtual reality	Virtual Reality is an environment that is simulated by a computer. Most virtual reality environments are primarily visual experiences.
Wolpe	Wolpe is best known for applying classical conditioning principles to the treatment of phobias, called systematic desensitization. Any "neutral" stimulus, simple or complex that happens to make an impact on an individual at about the time that a fear reaction is evoked acquires the ability to evoke fear subsequently. An acquired CS-CR relationship should be extinguishable.
Simulation	A simulation is an imitation of some real device or state of affairs. Simulation attempts to represent certain features of the behavior of a physical or abstract system by the behavior of another system.
Exposure therapy	An exposure therapy is any method of treating fears, including flooding and systematic desensitization, that involves exposing the client to the feared object or situation so that the process of extinction or habituation of the fear response can occur.
American Psychological Association	The American Psychological Association is a professional organization representing psychology in the US. The mission statement is to "advance psychology as a science and profession and as a means of promoting health, education , and human welfare".
Control group	A group that does not receive the treatment effect in an experiment is referred to as the control group or sometimes as the comparison group.
Post-traumatic stress disorder	Post-traumatic stress disorder is a term for the psychological consequences of exposure to or confrontation with stressful experiences, which involve actual or threatened death, serious physical injury or a threat to physical integrity and which the person found highly traumatic.
Skinner	Skinner conducted research on shaping behavior through positive and negative reinforcement, and demonstrated operant conditioning, a technique which he developed in contrast with classical conditioning.
Estes	Estes proposed the Stimulus sampling theory as an attempt to develop a statistical explanation for learning phenomena. A key feature of SST was the probability of a certain stimulus occurring in any trial and of being paired with a given response. While learning of a particular instance is all or none, the overall learning process is gradual and cumulative.
Conditioned suppression	Conditioned suppression refers to a reduction in the rate of responding due to the presence of an aversive CS.
Conditional stimulus	A conditional stimulus in a conditional reflex elicits a conditional response.
Suppression	Suppression is the defense mechanism where a memory is deliberately forgotten.
Prejudice	Prejudice in general, implies coming to a judgment on the subject before learning where the preponderance of the evidence actually lies, or formation of a judgement without direct experience.
Affect	A subjective feeling or emotional tone often accompanied by bodily expressions noticeable to others is called affect.
Higher-order	In classical conditioning a neutral stimulus comes to elicit a condtioned response(CR)

conditioning	through repeated pairings of the neutral stimulus with a natural or unconditioned stimulus that results in that response. The nuetral stimulus is now called a conditioned stimulus(CS). That CS can also be paired with another nuetral stimulus to produce a higher-order conditioning; a chain of CS-CR relationships.
Ethnic group	An ethnic group is a culture or subculture whose members are readily distinguishable by outsiders based on traits originating from a common racial, national, linguistic, or religious source. Members of an ethnic group are often presumed to be culturally or biologically similar, although this is not in fact necessarily the case.
Acquisition	Acquisition is the process of adapting to the environment, learning or becoming conditioned. In classical conditoning terms, it is the initial learning of the stimulus response link, which involves a neutral stimulus being associated with a unconditioned stimulus and becoming a conditioned stimulus.
Fetal damage	Fetal damage refers to a congenital problem; that is, damage or injury that occurs to the fetus during prenatal development.
Alcoholism	A disorder that involves long-term, repeated, uncontrolled, compulsive, and excessive use of alcoholic beverages and that impairs the drinker's health and work and social relationships is called alcoholism.
Date rape	Date rape refers to non-consensual sexual activity between people who are already acquainted, or who know each other socially where it is alleged that consent for sexual activity was not given, or was given under duress.
Gonorrhea	Gonorrhea is among the most common curable sexually transmitted diseases in the world. In men, epididymitis, prostatitis and urethral stricture can result from untreated gonorrhoea.In women, Bartholinitis and abscess formation, pelvic inflammatory disease and Fitz-Hugh-Curtis syndrome can occur.
Sigmund Freud	Sigmund Freud was the founder of the psychoanalytic school, based on his theory that unconscious motives control much behavior, that particular kinds of unconscious thoughts and memories are the source of neurosis, and that neurosis could be treated through bringing these unconscious thoughts and memories to consciousness in psychoanalytic treatment.
Exhibitionism	Marked preference for obtaining sexual gratification by exposing one's genitals to an unwilling observer is called exhibitionism.
Pedophilia	Pedophilia is the condition of being sexually attracted primarily or exclusively to prepubescent children.
Voyeurism	Voyeurism is a practice in which an individual derives sexual pleasure from observing other people. Such people may be engaged in sexual acts, or be nude or in underwear, or dressed in whatever other way the "voyeur" finds appealing.
Fetishism	Sexual fetishism, first described as such by Alfred Binet in his Le fétichisme dans l'amour, though the concept and certainly the activity is quite ancient, is a form of paraphilia where the object of affection is a specific inanimate object or part of a person's body.
Masochism	The counterpart of sadism is masochism, the sexual pleasure or gratification of having pain or suffering inflicted upon the self, often consisting of sexual fantasies or urges for being beaten, humiliated, bound, tortured, or otherwise made to suffer, either as an enhancement to or a substitute for sexual pleasure.
Genitals	Genitals refers to the internal and external reproductive organs.
Society	The social sciences use the term society to mean a group of people that form a semi-closed (or semi-open) social system, in which most interactions are with other individuals belonging to the group.

Go to **Cram101.com** for the Practice Tests for this Chapter.

Sadism	Sadism is the sexual pleasure or gratification in the infliction of pain and suffering upon another person. It is considered to be a paraphilia. The word is derived from the name of the Marquis de Sade, a prolific French writer of sadistic novels.
Rape	Rape is a crime where the victim is forced into sexual activity, in particular sexual penetration, against his or her will.
Survey	A method of scientific investigation in which a large sample of people answer questions about their attitudes or behavior is referred to as a survey.
Abnormal behavior	An action, thought, or feeling that is harmful to the person or to others is called abnormal behavior.
Homosexuality	Homosexuality refers to a sexual orientation characterized by aesthetic attraction, romantic love, and sexual desire exclusively for members of the same sex or gender identity.
Plato	According to Plato, people must come equipped with most of their knowledge and need only hints and contemplation to complete it. Plato suggested that the brain is the mechanism of mental processes and that one gained knowledge by reflecting on the contents of one's mind.
Aversion therapy	Aversion therapy is a now largely discredited form of treatment in which the patient is exposed to a stimulus while simultaneously being hurt or made ill. The theory is that the patient will come to associate the stimulus with unpleasant sensations and will no longer seek it out.
Case study	A carefully drawn biography that may be obtained through interviews, questionnaires, and psychological tests is called a case study.
Masturbation	Masturbation is the manual excitation of the sexual organs, most often to the point of orgasm. It can refer to excitation either by oneself or by another, but commonly refers to such activities performed alone.
Adolescence	The period of life bounded by puberty and the assumption of adult responsibilities is adolescence.
Covert sensitization	A form of aversion therapy in which the person is told to imagine undesirably attractive situations and activities while unpleasant feelings are being induced by imagery is covert sensitization.
Morphine	Morphine, the principal active agent in opium, is a powerful opioid analgesic drug. According to recent research, it may also be produced naturally by the human brain. Morphine is usually highly addictive, and tolerance and physical and psychological dependence develop quickly.
Castration	Castration is any action, surgical, chemical or otherwise, by which a biological male loses use of the testes. This causes sterilization, i.e. prevents him from reproducing; it also greatly reduces the production of certain hormones, such as testosterone.
Testosterone	Testosterone is a steroid hormone from the androgen group. It is the principal male sex hormone and the "original" anabolic steroid.
Innate	Innate behavior is not learned or influenced by the environment, rather, it is present or predisposed at birth.
Locke	In 1690, Locke wrote his Essay Concerning Human Understanding. The essay arugued for empiricism, that ideas come only from experience. In other words, there are no innate ideas. The tabula rasa or blank slate was his metaphor.
Conditioned taste aversion	A procedure in which an animal drinks a flavored solution and is then made sick by a toxin is conditioned taste aversion, called the Garcia Effect. Both the long time interval between CS and CR and that only a single trial is necessary for the conditioning challenges normal conditioning tenets.

Latent inhibition	If after the habituation of a stimulus, it is later paired with a US the conditioning may be weak and unstable. This effect is called latent inhibition.
Alcoholic	An alcoholic is dependent on alcohol as characterized by craving, loss of control, physical dependence and withdrawal symptoms, and tolerance.
Chemotherapy	Chemotherapy is the use of chemical substances to treat disease. In its modern-day use, it refers almost exclusively to cytostatic drugs used to treat cancer. In its non-oncological use, the term may also refer to antibiotics.
Population	Population refers to all members of a well-defined group of organisms, events, or things.
Conservation	Conservation refers to the recognition that basic properties of substances such as weight and mass remain the same even when transformations merely alter their appearance.
Lithium	Lithium salts are used as mood stabilizing drugs primarily in the treatment of bipolar disorder, depression, and mania; but also in treating schizophrenia. Lithium is widely distributed in the central nervous system and interacts with a number of neurotransmitters and receptors, decreasing noradrenaline release and increasing serotonin synthesis.
Basic research	Basic research has as its primary objective the advancement of knowledge and the theoretical understanding of the relations among variables . It is exploratory and often driven by the researcher's curiosity, interest or hunch.
Immune system	The most important function of the human immune system occurs at the cellular level of the blood and tissues. The lymphatic and blood circulation systems are highways for specialized white blood cells. These cells include B cells, T cells, natural killer cells, and macrophages. All function with the primary objective of recognizing, attacking and destroying bacteria, viruses, cancer cells, and all substances seen as foreign.
Neutral stimulus	A stimulus prior to conditioning that does not naturally result in the response of interest is called a neutral stimulus.
Immune response	The body's defensive reaction to invasion by bacteria, viral agents, or other foreign substances is called the immune response.
Correlation	A statistical technique for determining the degree of association between two or more variables is referred to as correlation.
Dementia	Dementia is progressive decline in cognitive function due to damage or disease in the brain beyond what might be expected from normal aging.
Individuality	According to Cooper, individuality consists of two dimensions: self-assertion and separateness.
Gland	A gland is an organ in an animal's body that synthesizes a substance for release such as hormones, often into the bloodstream or into cavities inside the body or its outer surface.
Brain	The brain controls and coordinates most movement, behavior and homeostatic body functions such as heartbeat, blood pressure, fluid balance and body temperature. Functions of the brain are responsible for cognition, emotion, memory, motor learning and other sorts of learning. The brain is primarily made up of two types of cells: glia and neurons.
Psychosomatic	A psychosomatic illness is one with physical manifestations and perhaps a supposed psychological cause. It is often diagnosed when any known or identifiable physical cause was excluded by medical examination.
John Watson	John Watson, the father of behaviorism, developed the term "Behaviorism" as a name for his proposal to revolutionize the study of human psychology in order to put it on a firm experimental footing.

Aversive stimulus	A stimulus that elicits pain, fear, or avoidance is an aversive stimulus.

40

Go to **Cram101.com** for the Practice Tests for this Chapter.

Psychic reflex	Pavlov called the association between a conditioned stimulus and the conditioned response a psychic reflex or a conditional reflex. It was psychic because it was not the result of the physiological makeup of the animal. It was conditional, because past experiences set a kind of rule that "if this happens, then that will follow."
Thorndike	Thorndike worked in animal behavior and the learning process leading to the theory of connectionism. Among his most famous contributions were his research on cats escaping from puzzle boxes, and his formulation of the Law of Effect.
Pavlov	Pavlov first described the phenomenon now known as classical conditioning in experiments with dogs.
Reasoning	Reasoning is the act of using reason to derive a conclusion from certain premises. There are two main methods to reach a conclusion,deductive reasoning and inductive reasoning.
Anecdotal evidence	Anecdotal evidence is unreliable evidence based on personal experience that has not been empirically tested, and which is often used in an argument as if it had been scientifically or statistically proven. The person using anecdotal evidence may or may not be aware of the fact that, by doing so, they are generalizing.
Reinforcement	In operant conditioning, reinforcement is any change in an environment that (a) occurs after the behavior, (b) seems to make that behavior re-occur more often in the future and (c) that reoccurence of behavior must be the result of the change.
Puzzle Box	The puzzle box experiments were motivated in part by Thorndike's dislike for statements that animals made use of extraordinary factulties such as insight in their problem solving. He reasoned that if the animals were showing insight, then their time to escape would suddenly drop to a negligible period, which would also be shown in the learning curve as an abrupt drop; while animals using a more ordinary method of trial and error would show gradual curves. His finding was that cats consistently showed gradual learning. He asserted that the connection between the box and the motions the cat used to escape was strengthened by each escape.
Learning	Learning is a relatively permanent change in behavior that results from experience. Thus, to attribute a behavioral change to learning, the change must be relatively permanent and must result from experience.
Hedonism	The motivation of humans and other animals to seek pleasure and avoid pain is referred to as hedonism.
Attention	Attention is the cognitive process of selectively concentrating on one thing while ignoring other things. Psychologists have labeled three types of attention: sustained attention, selective attention, and divided attention.
Law of effect	The law of effect is a principle of psychology described by Edward Thorndike in 1898. It holds that responses to stimuli that produce a satisfying or pleasant effect in a particular situation are more likely to occur again in the situation. Conversely, responses that produce a discomforting or unpleasant effect are less likely to occur again in the situation
Nervous system	The body's electrochemical communication circuitry, made up of billions of neurons is a nervous system.
Cognitive science	Cognitive Science is the scientific study of the mind and brain and how they give rise to behavior. The field is highly interdisciplinary and is closely related to several other areas, including psychology, artificial intelligence, linguistics and psycholinguistics, philosophy, neuroscience, logic, robotics, anthropology and biology.
Skinner box	An operant conditioning chamber, or Skinner box, is an experimental apparatus used to study conditioning in animals. Chambers have at least one operandum that can automatically detect

the occurrence of a behavioral response or action. The other minimal requirement of a conditioning chamber is that it have a means of delivering a primary reinforcer or unconditioned stimulus like food or water.

Skinner	Skinner conducted research on shaping behavior through positive and negative reinforcement, and demonstrated operant conditioning, a technique which he developed in contrast with classical conditioning.
Operant learning	A simple form of learning in which an organism learns to engage in behavior because it is reinforced is referred to as operant learning. The consequences of a behavior produce changes in the probability of the behavior's occurence.
Hull	Hull is best known for the Drive Reduction Theory which postulated that behavior occurs in response to primary drives such as hunger, thirst, sexual interest, etc. When the goal of the drive is attained the drive is reduced. This reduction of drive serves as a reinforcer for learning.
Pavlovian conditioning	Pavlovian conditioning, synonymous with classical conditioning is a type of learning found in animals, caused by the association (or pairing) of two stimuli or what Ivan Pavlov described as the learning of conditional behavior, therefore called conditioning.
Operant chamber	An operant chamber (usually Skinner box) is a laboratory apparatus used in experimental psychology to study animal behavior. It is used to study both classical conditioning (especially autoshaping) and operant conditioning.
Cognition	The intellectual processes through which information is obtained, transformed, stored, retrieved, and otherwise used is cognition.
Conditioning	Conditioning describes the process by which behaviors can be learned or modified through interaction with the environment.
Stimulus	A change in an environmental condition that elicits a response is a stimulus.
Reflex	A simple, involuntary response to a stimulus is referred to as reflex. Reflex actions originate at the spinal cord rather than the brain.
William James	Functionalism as a psychology developed out of Pragmatism as a philosophy: To find the meaning of an idea, you have to look at its consequences. This led William James and his students towards an emphasis on cause and effect, prediction and control, and observation of environment and behavior, over the careful introspection of the Structuralists.
Educational psychology	Educational psychology is the study of how children and adults learn, the effectiveness of various educational strategies and tactics, and how schools function as organizations.
Psychological testing	Psychological testing is a field characterized by the use of small samples of behavior in order to infer larger generalizations about a given individual. The technical term for psychological testing is psychometrics.
Positive reinforcement	In positive reinforcement, a stimulus is added and the rate of responding increases.
Positive reinforcer	In operant conditioning, a stimulus that is presented after a response that increases the likelihood that the response will be repeated is a positive reinforcer.
Negative reinforcement	During negative reinforcement, a stimulus is removed and the frequency of the behavior or response increases.
Reinforcer	In operant conditioning, a reinforcer is any stimulus that increases the probability that a preceding behavior will occur again. In Classical Conditioning, the unconditioned stimulus (US) is the reinforcer.

Go to **Cram101.com** for the Practice Tests for this Chapter.

Aversive stimulus	A stimulus that elicits pain, fear, or avoidance is an aversive stimulus.
Darwin	Darwin achieved lasting fame as originator of the theory of evolution through natural selection. His book Expression of Emotions in Man and Animals is generally considered the first text on comparative psychology.
American Psychological Association	The American Psychological Association is a professional organization representing psychology in the US. The mission statement is to "advance psychology as a science and profession and as a means of promoting health, education , and human welfare".
Principles of Behavior	Hull published Principles of Behavior, in 1943. His theory is characterized by very strict operationalization of variables and mathematical presentation. The essence of the theory can be summarized by saying that the response is a function of the strength of the habit times the strength of the drive. It is for this reason that Hull's theory is often referred to as drive theory.
Dependent variable	A measure of an assumed effect of an independent variable is called the dependent variable.
Free operant procedure	A free operant procedure is a training procedure in which a behavior may be repeated any number of times.
Variable	A variable refers to a measurable factor, characteristic, or attribute of an individual or a system.
Field experiment	A field experiment applies the scientific method to experimentally examine an intervention in the real world rather than in the laboratory. Field experiments generally randomize subjects into treatment and control groups and compare outcomes between these groups.
Natural selection	Natural selection is a process by which biological populations are altered over time, as a result of the propagation of heritable traits that affect the capacity of individual organisms to survive and reproduce.
Autonomic nervous system	A division of the peripheral nervous system, the autonomic nervous system, regulates glands and activities such as heartbeat, respiration, digestion, and dilation of the pupils. It is responsible for homeostasis, maintaining a relatively constant internal environment .
Trial and error	Trial and error is an approach to problem solving in which one solution after another is tried in no particular order until an answer is found.
Skeletal muscle	Skeletal muscle is a type of striated muscle, attached to the skeleton. They are used to facilitate movement, by applying force to bones and joints; via contraction. They generally contract voluntarily (via nerve stimulation), although they can contract involuntarily.
Gland	A gland is an organ in an animal's body that synthesizes a substance for release such as hormones, often into the bloodstream or into cavities inside the body or its outer surface.
Secondary Reinforcer	A conditioned reinforcer, sometimes called a secondary reinforcer, is a stimulus or situation that has acquired reinforcing power after being paired in the environment with an unconditioned reinforcer or an earlier conditioned reinforcer.
Primary Reinforcer	Any stimulus whose reinforcing effect is immediate and not a function of previous experience is a primary reinforcer (eg, food, water, warmth).
Learned helplessness	Learned helplessness is a description of the effect of inescapable positive punishment (such as electrical shock) on animal (and by extension, human) behavior.
Depression	In everyday language depression refers to any downturn in mood, which may be relatively transitory and perhaps due to something trivial. This is differentiated from Clinical depression which is marked by symptoms that last two weeks or more and are so severe that

Go to **Cram101.com** for the Practice Tests for this Chapter.

they interfere with daily living.

Conditioned reinforcer	A conditioned reinforcer is a stimulus or situation that has acquired reinforcing power after being paired in the environment with an unconditioned reinforcer or an earlier conditioned reinforcer.
Morphine	Morphine, the principal active agent in opium, is a powerful opioid analgesic drug. According to recent research, it may also be produced naturally by the human brain. Morphine is usually highly addictive, and tolerance and physical and psychological dependence develop quickly.
Generalized reinforcer	Generalized reinforcer refers to any secondary reinforcer that has been paired with several different primary reinforcers.
Confederate	Someone who is posing as a participant in an experiment but is actually assisting the experimenter is a confederate.
Innate	Innate behavior is not learned or influenced by the environment, rather, it is present or predisposed at birth.
Chaining	Chaining involves reinforcing individual responses occurring in a sequence to form a complex behavior. It is frequently used for training behavioral sequences that are beyond the current repetoire of the learner.
Shaping	The concept of reinforcing successive, increasingly accurate approximations to a target behavior is called shaping. The target behavior is broken down into a hierarchy of elemental steps, each step more sophisticated then the last. By successively reinforcing each of the the elemental steps, a form of differential reinforcement, until that step is learned while extinguishing the step below, the target behavior is gradually achieved.
Habit	A habit is a response that has become completely separated from its eliciting stimulus. Early learning theorists used the term to describe S-R associations, however not all S-R associations become a habit, rather many are extinguished after reinforcement is withdrawn.
Successive approximations	In operant conditioning, a series of behaviors that gradually become more similar to a target behavior are called successive approximations.
Obedience	Obedience is the willingness to follow the will of others. Humans have been shown to be surprisingly obedient in the presence of perceived legitimate authority figures, as demonstrated by the Milgram experiment in the 1960s.
Variability	Statistically, variability refers to how much the scores in a distribution spread out, away from the mean.
Temperament	Temperament refers to a basic, innate disposition to change behavior. The activity level is an important dimension of temperament.
Trait	An enduring personality characteristic that tends to lead to certain behaviors is called a trait. The term trait also means a genetically inherited feature of an organism.
Behavior chain	A series of related behaviors, the last of which is followed by reinforcement is a behavior chain.
Task analysis	The procedure of identifying the component elements of a behavior chain is called task analysis.
Backward chaining	Backward chaining starts with a list of goals and works backwards to see if there is data which will allow it to conclude any of these goals.
Forward chaining	Forward chaining starts with the available data and uses inference rules to extract more data (from an end user for example) until an optimal goal is reached.
Correlation	A statistical technique for determining the degree of association between two or more

variables is referred to as correlation.

Rescorla	Rescorla agreed with Pavlov that for learning to take place, the CS had to be a useful predictor of the US. But he disagreed on what made the CS a useful predictor. It was more complicated than the number of CS-US pairings. He maintained that it was the contingency between the CS and US.
Response rate	The response rate is usually calculated by dividing the total number of responses by the time available for the response.
Delay of reinforcement	The amount of time between the response and the reinforcement, which may effect the acquisition of the association of stimulus and response, is called delay of reinforcement. Generally, the greater the delay, the greater the time to acquisition.
Hypothesis	A specific statement about behavior or mental processes that is testable through research is a hypothesis.
Affect	A subjective feeling or emotional tone often accompanied by bodily expressions noticeable to others is called affect.
Reid	Reid was the founder of the Scottish School of Common Sense, and played an integral role in the Scottish Enlightenment. He advocated direct realism, or common sense realism, and argued strongly against the Theory of Ideas advocated by John Locke and René Descartes.
Smooth muscle	Smooth muscle is a type of non-striated muscle, found within the "walls" of hollow organs, such as blood vessels, the bladder, the uterus, and the gastrointestinal tract. Smooth muscle is used to move matter within the body, via contraction; it generally operates "involuntarily", without nerve stimulation.
Biofeedback	Biofeedback is the process of measuring and quantifying an aspect of a subject's physiology, analyzing the data, and then feeding back the information to the subject in a form that allows the subject to enact physiological change.
Neal Miller	Neal Miller introduced the concepts of the approach gradient and avoidance gradient. Whether organisms drive toward or away from a positive stimulus or a negative stimulus is a function of the distance that it is from that stimulus.
Migraine	Migraine is a form of headache, usually very intense and disabling. It is a neurologic disease.
Deprivation	Deprivation, is the loss or withholding of normal stimulation, nutrition, comfort, love, and so forth; a condition of lacking. The level of stimulation is less than what is required.
Individual differences	Individual differences psychology studies the ways in which individual people differ in their behavior. This is distinguished from other aspects of psychology in that although psychology is ostensibly a study of individuals, modern psychologists invariably study groups.
Individuality	According to Cooper, individuality consists of two dimensions: self-assertion and separateness.
Tolman	Tolman coined the term "cognitive map", which was an internal perceptual representation of external environmental features and landmarks. He is virtually the only behaviorist who found the Stimulus-Response theory unacceptable, because reinforcement was not necessary for learning to occur. He felt behavior was holistic, purposive, and cognitive.
Heredity	Heredity is the transfer of characteristics from parent to offspring through their genes.
Trial-and-error learning	Learning that occurs when a response is associated with a successful solution to a problem after a number of unsuccessful responses is referred to as trial-and-error learning.
Herrnstein	Herrnstein was a prominent researcher in comparative psychology who did pioneering work on

Go to **Cram101.com** for the Practice Tests for this Chapter.

pigeon intelligence employing the Experimental Analysis of Behavior and formulated the "Matching Law" in the 1960s, a breakthrough in understanding how reinforcement and behavior are linked.

Classical conditioning	Classical conditioning is a simple form of learning in which an organism comes to associate or anticipate events. A neutral stimulus comes to evoke the response usually evoked by a natural or unconditioned stimulus by being paired repeatedly with the unconditioned stimulus.
Extinction	In operant extinction, if no reinforcement is delivered after the response, gradually the behavior will no longer occur in the presence of the stimulus. The process is more rapid following continuous reinforcement rather than after partial reinforcement. In Classical Conditioning, repeated presentations of the CS without being followed by the US results in the extinction of the CS.
Extinction burst	A sudden increase in the rate of behavior during the early stages of extinction is called an extinction burst.
Resurgence	Resurgence refers to the reappearance during extinction, of a previously reinforced behavior.
Regression	Return to a form of behavior characteristic of an earlier stage of development is called regression.
Clinician	A health professional authorized to provide services to people suffering from one or more pathologies is a clinician.
Spontaneous recovery	The recurrence of an extinguished response as a function of the passage of time is referred to as spontaneous recovery.
Theories	Theories are logically self-consistent models or frameworks describing the behavior of a certain natural or social phenomenon. They are broad explanations and predictions concerning phenomena of interest.
Feedback	Feedback refers to information returned to a person about the effects a response has had.
Median	The median is a number that separates the higher half of a sample, a population, or a probability distribution from the lower half. It is the middle value in a distribution, above and below which lie an equal number of values.
Motivational state	A motivational state is an internal, reversible condition in an individual that orients the individual toward one or another type of goal. This condition is not observed directly but is inferred from the individual's behavior.
Drive-reduction	Drive-reduction theories are based on the need-state. Drive activates behavior. Reinforcement occurs whenever drive is reduced, leading to learning of whatever response solves the need. Thus the reduction in need serves as reinforcement and produces reinforcement of the response that leads to it.
Positive feedback	When a change in a variable occurs in a system, the system responds. In the case of positive feedback the response of the system is to cause that variable to increase in the same direction.
Drive reduction	Drive reduction theories are based on the need-state. Drive activates behavior. Reinforcement occurs whenever drive is reduced, leading to learning of whatever response solves the need. Thus the reduction in need serves as reinforcement and produces reinforcement of the response that leads to it.
Ejaculation	Ejaculation is the process of ejecting semen from the penis, and is usually accompanied by orgasm as a result of sexual stimulation.
Relative value theory	The relative value theory of reinforcement considers reinforcers to be behaviors rather than stimuli. It attributes a reinforcer's effectiveness to its probability relative to other

behaviors.

Premack principle	That any high-frequency response can be used to reinforce a low-frequency response is called the Premack Principle.
Generalization	In conditioning, the tendency for a conditioned response to be evoked by stimuli that are similar to the stimulus to which the response was conditioned is a generalization. The greater the similarity among the stimuli, the greater the probability of generalization.
Reinforcement value	The reinforcement value is the strength of the rate of responding or the intensity of the response.
Empirical	Empirical means the use of working hypotheses which are capable of being disproved using observation or experiment.
Timberlake	Timberlake and his Biological Psychology argues that you cannot neglect species-specific differences in prepared behaviors when discussing learning.
Equilibrium Theory	The basic idea behind Timberlake and Allison's Equilibrium Theory is that animals in a free choice situation are in a state of equilibrium: They are able to engage in various activities at their preferred levels.
Baseline	Measure of a particular behavior or process taken before the introduction of the independent variable or treatment is called the baseline.
One-process theory	The one-process theory is the view that avoidance and punishment involve only one procedure, operant learning.
Stages	Stages represent relatively discrete periods of time in which functioning is qualitatively different from functioning at other periods.
Kamin	Kamin argues that blocking is caused by lack of learning. In the compound stimulus training, there is lack of surprise about the outcome because one of the members of the compound stimulus already predicts the outcome. There is no surprise effect, therefore no learning.
Avoidance learning	Avoidance learning describes how a learner develops a pattern that will allow him/her to avoid an aversive location or situation. Avoidance learning takes place when a map is created which allows the learner not to go to the place where the aversive is.
Evolution	Commonly used to refer to gradual change, evolution is the change in the frequency of alleles within a population from one generation to the next. This change may be caused by different mechanisms, including natural selection, genetic drift, or changes in population (gene flow).
Analogy	An analogy is a comparison between two different things, in order to highlight some form of similarity. Analogy is the cognitive process of transferring information from a particular subject to another particular subject.
Problem solving	An attempt to find an appropriate way of attaining a goal when the goal is not readily available is called problem solving.
Sternberg	Sternberg proposed the triarchic theory of intelligence: componential, experiential, and practical. His notion of general intelligence or the g-factor, is a composite of intelligence scores across multiple modalities.
Brain	The brain controls and coordinates most movement, behavior and homeostatic body functions such as heartbeat, blood pressure, fluid balance and body temperature. Functions of the brain are responsible for cognition, emotion, memory, motor learning and other sorts of learning. The brain is primarily made up of two types of cells: glia and neurons.
Incentive	An incentive is what is expected once a behavior is performed. An incentive acts as a reinforcer.

Reinforcement	In operant conditioning, reinforcement is any change in an environment that (a) occurs after the behavior, (b) seems to make that behavior re-occur more often in the future and (c) that reoccurence of behavior must be the result of the change.
Positive reinforcement	In positive reinforcement, a stimulus is added and the rate of responding increases.
Punishment	Punishment is the addtion of a stimulus that reduces the frequency of a response, or the removal of a stimulus that results in a reduction of the response.
Punisher	Punisher refers to any event that decreases the probability or frequency of the response it follows.
Reinforcer	In operant conditioning, a reinforcer is any stimulus that increases the probability that a preceding behavior will occur again. In Classical Conditioning, the unconditioned stimulus (US) is the reinforcer.
Negative reinforcement	During negative reinforcement, a stimulus is removed and the frequency of the behavior or response increases.
Positive punishment	In operant conditioning, when the presentation of a stimulus after a response occurs decreases the likelihood that the response will be repeated, you have positive punishment.
Negative punishment	Negative punishment occurs when a response decreases as a positive stimulus is removed from the situation.
Stimulus	A change in an environmental condition that elicits a response is a stimulus.
Learning	Learning is a relatively permanent change in behavior that results from experience. Thus, to attribute a behavioral change to learning, the change must be relatively permanent and must result from experience.
Variable	A variable refers to a measurable factor, characteristic, or attribute of an individual or a system.
Physiological psychology	Physiological psychology refers to the study of the physiological mechanisms, in the brain and elsewhere, that mediate behavior and psychological experiences.
Response-contingent	Reinforcement, punishment, or other consequences that are applied only when a certain response is made are response-contingent consequences.
Extinction	In operant extinction, if no reinforcement is delivered after the response, gradually the behavior will no longer occur in the presence of the stimulus. The process is more rapid following continuous reinforcement rather than after partial reinforcement. In Classical Conditioning, repeated presentations of the CS without being followed by the US results in the extinction of the CS.
Median	The median is a number that separates the higher half of a sample, a population, or a probability distribution from the lower half. It is the middle value in a distribution, above and below which lie an equal number of values.
Control group	A group that does not receive the treatment effect in an experiment is referred to as the control group or sometimes as the comparison group.
Suppression	Suppression is the defense mechanism where a memory is deliberately forgotten.
Skinner	Skinner conducted research on shaping behavior through positive and negative reinforcement, and demonstrated operant conditioning, a technique which he developed in contrast with classical conditioning.
Thorndike	Thorndike worked in animal behavior and the learning process leading to the theory of connectionism. Among his most famous contributions were his research on cats escaping from

	puzzle boxes, and his formulation of the Law of Effect.
Neal Miller	Neal Miller introduced the concepts of the approach gradient and avoidance gradient. Whether organisms drive toward or away from a positive stimulus or a negative stimulus is a function of the distance that it is from that stimulus.
Abnormal behavior	An action, thought, or feeling that is harmful to the person or to others is called abnormal behavior.
Attention	Attention is the cognitive process of selectively concentrating on one thing while ignoring other things. Psychologists have labeled three types of attention: sustained attention, selective attention, and divided attention.
Deprivation	Deprivation, is the loss or withholding of normal stimulation, nutrition, comfort, love, and so forth; a condition of lacking. The level of stimulation is less than what is required.
Affect	A subjective feeling or emotional tone often accompanied by bodily expressions noticeable to others is called affect.
Theories	Theories are logically self-consistent models or frameworks describing the behavior of a certain natural or social phenomenon. They are broad explanations and predictions concerning phenomena of interest.
Guthrie	The theory of learning proposed by Guthrie was based on one principle, Contiguity : A combination of stimuli which has accompanied a movement will on its recurrence tend to be followed by that movement. Prediction of behavior will always be probabilistic.
Estes	Estes proposed the Stimulus sampling theory as an attempt to develop a statistical explanation for learning phenomena. A key feature of SST was the probability of a certain stimulus occurring in any trial and of being paired with a given response. While learning of a particular instance is all or none, the overall learning process is gradual and cumulative.
Avoidance learning	Avoidance learning describes how a learner develops a pattern that will allow him/her to avoid an aversive location or situation. Avoidance learning takes place when a map is created which allows the learner not to go to the place where the aversive is.
Pavlovian conditioning	Pavlovian conditioning, synonymous with classical conditioning is a type of learning found in animals, caused by the association (or pairing) of two stimuli or what Ivan Pavlov described as the learning of conditional behavior, therefore called conditioning.
One-process theory	The one-process theory is the view that avoidance and punishment involve only one procedure, operant learning.
Operant learning	A simple form of learning in which an organism learns to engage in behavior because it is reinforced is referred to as operant learning. The consequences of a behavior produce changes in the probability of the behavior's occurence.
Premack principle	That any high-frequency response can be used to reinforce a low-frequency response is called the Premack Principle.
Suicide	Suicide behavior is rare in childhood but escalates in adolescence. The suicide rate increases in a linear fashion from adolescence through late adulthood.
Ethnic group	An ethnic group is a culture or subculture whose members are readily distinguishable by outsiders based on traits originating from a common racial, national, linguistic, or religious source. Members of an ethnic group are often presumed to be culturally or biologically similar, although this is not in fact necessarily the case.
Positive reinforcer	In operant conditioning, a stimulus that is presented after a response that increases the likelihood that the response will be repeated is a positive reinforcer.

Corporal punishment	Corporal punishment is the use of physical force with the intention of causing pain, but not injury.
Child abuse	Child abuse is the physical or psychological maltreatment of a child.
Nerve	A nerve is an enclosed, cable-like bundle of nerve fibers or axons, which includes the glia that ensheath the axons in myelin. Neurons are sometimes called nerve cells, though this term is technically imprecise since many neurons do not form nerves.
Brain	The brain controls and coordinates most movement, behavior and homeostatic body functions such as heartbeat, blood pressure, fluid balance and body temperature. Functions of the brain are responsible for cognition, emotion, memory, motor learning and other sorts of learning. The brain is primarily made up of two types of cells: glia and neurons.
Bandura	Bandura is best known for his work on social learning theory or Social Cognitivism. His famous Bobo doll experiment illustrated that people learn from observing others.
Sears	Sears focused on the application of the social learning theory (SLT) to socialization processes, and how children internalize the values, attitudes, and behaviors predominant in their culture. He articulated the place of parents in fostering internalization. In addition, he was among the first social learning theorists to officially acknowledge the reciprocal interaction on an individual's behavior and their environment
Response prevention	Response prevention is a behavior therapy technique in which the person is discouraged from making an accustomed response, used primarily with compulsive rituals.
Extinction burst	A sudden increase in the rate of behavior during the early stages of extinction is called an extinction burst.
Differential reinforcement	Any training procedure in which certain kinds of behavior are systematically reinforced and others are not is called differential reinforcement. Differential reinforcement involves both reinforcement and extinction.
Noncontingent reinforcement	Noncontingent reinforcement refers to the procedure of providing reinforcers independently of behavior.
Functional communication training	Functional communication training is the teaching of speech or nonspeech skills to replace some undesired behavior. The new skills are useful to the person and will be maintained because of the positve effects they have on others and on the individual.
Operant behavior	Operant behavior is simply emitted by an organism, that is, all organisms are inherently active, emitting responses that operate in the environment. Unlike respondent behavior, which is dependent on the stimulus that preceded it, operant behavior is a function of its consequences.

61

Learned helplessness	Learned helplessness is a description of the effect of inescapable positive punishment (such as electrical shock) on animal (and by extension, human) behavior.
Hallucination	A hallucination is a sensory perception experienced in the absence of an external stimulus, as distinct from an illusion, which is a misperception of an external stimulus. They may occur in any sensory modality - visual, auditory, olfactory, gustatory, tactile, or mixed.
Delusion	A false belief, not generally shared by others, and that cannot be changed despite strong evidence to the contrary is a delusion.
Positive reinforcement	In positive reinforcement, a stimulus is added and the rate of responding increases.
Conditioned reinforcer	A conditioned reinforcer is a stimulus or situation that has acquired reinforcing power after being paired in the environment with an unconditioned reinforcer or an earlier conditioned reinforcer.
Reinforcement	In operant conditioning, reinforcement is any change in an environment that (a) occurs after the behavior, (b) seems to make that behavior re-occur more often in the future and (c) that reoccurence of behavior must be the result of the change.
Shaping	The concept of reinforcing successive, increasingly accurate approximations to a target behavior is called shaping. The target behavior is broken down into a hierarchy of elemental steps, each step more sophisticated then the last. By successively reinforcing each of the the elemental steps, a form of differential reinforcement, until that step is learned while extinguishing the step below, the target behavior is gradually achieved.
Skinner	Skinner conducted research on shaping behavior through positive and negative reinforcement, and demonstrated operant conditioning, a technique which he developed in contrast with classical conditioning.
Temperament	Temperament refers to a basic, innate disposition to change behavior. The activity level is an important dimension of temperament.
Enrichment	Deliberately making an environment more novel, complex, and perceptually or intellectually stimulating is referred to as enrichment.
Learning	Learning is a relatively permanent change in behavior that results from experience. Thus, to attribute a behavioral change to learning, the change must be relatively permanent and must result from experience.
Self-awareness	Realization that one's existence and functioning are separate from those of other people and things is called self-awareness.
Separation anxiety	Separation anxiety is a psychological condition in which an individual has excessive anxiety regarding separation from home, or from those with whom the individual has a strong attachment.
Attention	Attention is the cognitive process of selectively concentrating on one thing while ignoring other things. Psychologists have labeled three types of attention: sustained attention, selective attention, and divided attention.
Stages	Stages represent relatively discrete periods of time in which functioning is qualitatively different from functioning at other periods.
Reflection	Reflection is the process of rephrasing or repeating thoughts and feelings expressed, making the person more aware of what they are saying or thinking.
Anesthesia	Anesthesia is the process of blocking the perception of pain and other sensations. This allows patients to undergo surgery and other procedures without the distress and pain they would otherwise experience.

Self-concept	Self-concept refers to domain-specific evaluations of the self where a domain may be academics, athletics, etc.
Deep sleep	Deep sleep refers to stage 4 sleep; the deepest form of normal sleep.
Operant learning	A simple form of learning in which an organism learns to engage in behavior because it is reinforced is referred to as operant learning. The consequences of a behavior produce changes in the probability of the behavior's occurence.
Successive approximations	In operant conditioning, a series of behaviors that gradually become more similar to a target behavior are called successive approximations.
Reinforcer	In operant conditioning, a reinforcer is any stimulus that increases the probability that a preceding behavior will occur again. In Classical Conditioning, the unconditioned stimulus (US) is the reinforcer.
Deprivation	Deprivation, is the loss or withholding of normal stimulation, nutrition, comfort, love, and so forth; a condition of lacking. The level of stimulation is less than what is required.
Affect	A subjective feeling or emotional tone often accompanied by bodily expressions noticeable to others is called affect.
Bandura	Bandura is best known for his work on social learning theory or Social Cognitivism. His famous Bobo doll experiment illustrated that people learn from observing others.
Mischel	Mischel is known for his cognitive social learning model of personality that focuses on the specific cognitive variables that mediate the manner in which new experiences affect the individual.
Human nature	Human nature is the fundamental nature and substance of humans, as well as the range of human behavior that is believed to be invariant over long periods of time and across very different cultural contexts.
Variable	A variable refers to a measurable factor, characteristic, or attribute of an individual or a system.
Verbal Behavior	Verbal Behavior is a book written by B.F. Skinner in which the author presents his ideas on language. For Skinner, speech, along with other forms of communication, was simply a behavior. Skinner argued that each act of speech is an inevitable consequence of the speaker's current environment and his behavioral and sensory history.
Thorndike	Thorndike worked in animal behavior and the learning process leading to the theory of connectionism. Among his most famous contributions were his research on cats escaping from puzzle boxes, and his formulation of the Law of Effect.
Survey	A method of scientific investigation in which a large sample of people answer questions about their attitudes or behavior is referred to as a survey.
Infancy	The developmental period that extends from birth to 18 or 24 months is called infancy.
Control subjects	Control subjects are participants in an experiment who do not receive the treatment effect but for whom all other conditions are held comparable to those of experimental subjects.
Control group	A group that does not receive the treatment effect in an experiment is referred to as the control group or sometimes as the comparison group.
Punishment	Punishment is the addtion of a stimulus that reduces the frequency of a response, or the removal of a stimulus that results in a reduction of the response.
Research design	A research design tests a hypothesis. The basic typess are: descriptive, correlational, and experimental.

Go to **Cram101.com** for the Practice Tests for this Chapter.

Baseline	Measure of a particular behavior or process taken before the introduction of the independent variable or treatment is called the baseline.
Early childhood	Early childhood refers to the developmental period extending from the end of infancy to about 5 or 6 years of age; sometimes called the preschool years.
Reinforcement contingencies	The circumstances or rules that determine whether responses lead to the presentation of reinforcers are referred to as reinforcement contingencies. Skinner defined culture as a set of reinforcement contingencies.
Sullivan	Sullivan developed the Self System, a configuration of the personality traits developed in childhood and reinforced by positive affirmation and the security operations developed in childhood to avoid anxiety and threats to self-esteem.
Feedback	Feedback refers to information returned to a person about the effects a response has had.
Nonverbal communication	Communication between individuals that does not involve the content of spoken language, but relies instead on an unspoken language of facial expressions, eye contact, and body language is nonverbal communication.
Ekman	Ekman found that at least some facial expressions and their corresponding emotions are not culturally determined, and thus presumably biological in origin. Expressions he found to be universal included anger, disgust, fear, joy, sadness and surprise.
Empirical	Empirical means the use of working hypotheses which are capable of being disproved using observation or experiment.
Problem solving	An attempt to find an appropriate way of attaining a goal when the goal is not readily available is called problem solving.
Insight	Insight refers to a sudden awareness of the relationships among various elements that had previously appeared to be independent of one another.
Kohler	Kohler applied Gestalt principles to study chimpanzees and recorded their ability to devise and use tools and solve problems. In 1917, he published and gained fame with The Mentality of Apes, in which he argued that his subjects, like humans, were capable of insight learning. His work led to a radical revision of learning theory.
Harlow	Harlow and his famous wire and cloth surrogate mother monkey studies demonstrated that the need for affection created a stronger bond between mother and infant than did physical needs. He also found that the more discrimination problems the monkeys solved, the better they became at solving them.
Bruner	Bruner has had an enormous impact on educational psychology with his contributions to cognitive learning theory. His ideas are based on categorization, maintaining that people interpret the world in terms of its similarities and differences.
Evolution	Commonly used to refer to gradual change, evolution is the change in the frequency of alleles within a population from one generation to the next. This change may be caused by different mechanisms, including natural selection, genetic drift, or changes in population (gene flow).
Darwin	Darwin achieved lasting fame as originator of the theory of evolution through natural selection. His book Expression of Emotions in Man and Animals is generally considered the first text on comparative psychology.
Retrieval	Retrieval is the location of stored information and its subsequent return to consciousness. It is the third stage of information processing.
Intuition	Quick, impulsive thought that does not make use of formal logic or clear reasoning is referred to as intuition.

Creativity	Creativity is the ability to think about something in novel and unusual ways and come up with unique solutions to problems. It involves divergent thinking, having many solutions or views to a problem.
Unconscious mind	The unconscious mind refers to information processing and brain functioning of which a person is unaware. In Freudian theory,it is the repository of unacceptable thoughts and feelings.
Pupil	In the eye, the pupil is the opening in the middle of the iris. It appears black because most of the light entering it is absorbed by the tissues inside the eye. The size of the pupil is controlled by involuntary contraction and dilation of the iris, in order to regulate the intensity of light entering the eye. This is known as the pupillary reflex.
Species	Species refers to a reproductively isolated breeding population.
Experimental group	Experimental group refers to any group receiving a treatment effect in an experiment.
Society	The social sciences use the term society to mean a group of people that form a semi-closed (or semi-open) social system, in which most interactions are with other individuals belonging to the group.
Variability	Statistically, variability refers to how much the scores in a distribution spread out, away from the mean.
Extinction	In operant extinction, if no reinforcement is delivered after the response, gradually the behavior will no longer occur in the presence of the stimulus. The process is more rapid following continuous reinforcement rather than after partial reinforcement. In Classical Conditioning, repeated presentations of the CS without being followed by the US results in the extinction of the CS.
Superstitious behavior	"When small amounts of food are repeatedly given, a 'superstitious ritual' may be set up. This is due not only to the fact that a reinforcing stimulus strengthens any behavior it may happen to follow, even though a contingency has not been explicitly arranged, but also to the fact that the change in behavior resulting from one accidental contingency makes similar accidents more probable."-- Skinner on superstitious behavior.
Fixed interval	In a fixed interval schedule of reinforcement, reinforcement occurs after the passage of a specified length of time from the beginning of training or from the last reinforcement, provided that at least one response occurred in that time period.
Herrnstein	Herrnstein was a prominent researcher in comparative psychology who did pioneering work on pigeon intelligence employing the Experimental Analysis of Behavior and formulated the "Matching Law" in the 1960s, a breakthrough in understanding how reinforcement and behavior are linked.
Hypothesis	A specific statement about behavior or mental processes that is testable through research is a hypothesis.
Negative reinforcement	During negative reinforcement, a stimulus is removed and the frequency of the behavior or response increases.
Reinforcement Theory	Reinforcement theory holds that reinforcers can control behavior. The definition has two main components: Contingency, where the occurrence of the reinforcer depends on the occurrence of the learner's response, and Rate of Responding, where the reinforcer serves to increase the learner's rate of responding.
Timberlake	Timberlake and his Biological Psychology argues that you cannot neglect species-specific differences in prepared behaviors when discussing learning.
Scientific	Psychologists gather data in order to describe, understand, predict, and control behavior.

method	Scientific method refers to an approach that can be used to discover accurate information. It includes these steps: understand the problem, collect data, draw conclusions, and revise research conclusions.
Escape learning	A type of learning in which an organism acquires a response that decreases or ends some aversive stimulation is referred to as escape learning.
Conditioning	Conditioning describes the process by which behaviors can be learned or modified through interaction with the environment.
Depression	In everyday language depression refers to any downturn in mood, which may be relatively transitory and perhaps due to something trivial. This is differentiated from Clinical depression which is marked by symptoms that last two weeks or more and are so severe that they interfere with daily living.
Behavior therapy	Behavior therapy refers to the systematic application of the principles of learning to direct modification of a client's problem behaviors.
Tranquilizer	A sedative, or tranquilizer, is a drug that depresses the central nervous system (CNS), which causes calmness, relaxation, reduction of anxiety, sleepiness, slowed breathing, slurred speech, staggering gait, poor judgment, and slow, uncertain reflexes.
Sympathetic	The sympathetic nervous system activates what is often termed the "fight or flight response". It is an automatic regulation system, that is, one that operates without the intervention of conscious thought.
Clinician	A health professional authorized to provide services to people suffering from one or more pathologies is a clinician.
Mental retardation	Mental retardation refers to having significantly below-average intellectual functioning and limitations in at least two areas of adaptive functioning. Many categorize retardation as mild, moderate, severe, or profound.
Autism	Autism is a neurodevelopmental disorder that manifests itself in markedly abnormal social interaction, communication ability, patterns of interests, and patterns of behavior.
Brain	The brain controls and coordinates most movement, behavior and homeostatic body functions such as heartbeat, blood pressure, fluid balance and body temperature. Functions of the brain are responsible for cognition, emotion, memory, motor learning and other sorts of learning. The brain is primarily made up of two types of cells: glia and neurons.
Stimulus control	Linking a particular response with specific stimuli is called stimulus control.
Differential reinforcement	Any training procedure in which certain kinds of behavior are systematically reinforced and others are not is called differential reinforcement. Differential reinforcement involves both reinforcement and extinction.
Symptom substitution	Psychodynamic assertion that if overt problem behavior is treated without eliminating the underlying conflict thought to be causing it, that conflict will reemerge in the form of new, perhaps worse, symptoms is symptom substitution.
Psychodynamic	Most psychodynamic approaches are centered around the idea of a maladapted function developed early in life (usually childhood) which are at least in part unconscious. This maladapted function (a.k.a. defense mechanism) does not do well in place of a normal/healthy one.
Etiology	Etiology is the study of causation. The term is used in philosophy, physics and biology in reference to the causes of various phenomena. It is generally the study of why things occur, or even the reasons behind the way that things act.
Mental illness	Mental illness is the term formerly used to mean psychological disorder but less preferred because it implies that the causes of the disorder can be found in a medical disease process.

Law of effect

The law of effect is a principle of psychology described by Edward Thorndike in 1898. It holds that responses to stimuli that produce a satisfying or pleasant effect in a particular situation are more likely to occur again in the situation. Conversely, responses that produce a discomforting or unpleasant effect are less likely to occur again in the situation

Classical conditioning	Classical conditioning is a simple form of learning in which an organism comes to associate or anticipate events. A neutral stimulus comes to evoke the response usually evoked by a natural or unconditioned stimulus by being paired repeatedly with the unconditioned stimulus.
Pavlov	Pavlov first described the phenomenon now known as classical conditioning in experiments with dogs.
Operant learning	A simple form of learning in which an organism learns to engage in behavior because it is reinforced is referred to as operant learning. The consequences of a behavior produce changes in the probability of the behavior's occurence.
Thorndike	Thorndike worked in animal behavior and the learning process leading to the theory of connectionism. Among his most famous contributions were his research on cats escaping from puzzle boxes, and his formulation of the Law of Effect.
Anecdotal evidence	Anecdotal evidence is unreliable evidence based on personal experience that has not been empirically tested, and which is often used in an argument as if it had been scientifically or statistically proven. The person using anecdotal evidence may or may not be aware of the fact that, by doing so, they are generalizing.
Puzzle Box	The puzzle box experiments were motivated in part by Thorndike's dislike for statements that animals made use of extraordinary factulties such as insight in their problem solving. He reasoned that if the animals were showing insight, then their time to escape would suddenly drop to a negligible period, which would also be shown in the learning curve as an abrupt drop; while animals using a more ordinary method of trial and error would show gradual curves. His finding was that cats consistently showed gradual learning. He asserted that the connection between the box and the motions the cat used to escape was strengthened by each escape.
Vicarious learning	Vicarious learning is learning without specific reinforcement for one's behavior. It is learning by observing others.
Modeling	A type of behavior learned through observation of others demonstrating the same behavior is modeling.
Bandura	Bandura is best known for his work on social learning theory or Social Cognitivism. His famous Bobo doll experiment illustrated that people learn from observing others.
Learning	Learning is a relatively permanent change in behavior that results from experience. Thus, to attribute a behavioral change to learning, the change must be relatively permanent and must result from experience.
Observational learning	The acquisition of knowledge and skills through the observation of others rather than by means of direct experience is observational learning. Four major processes are thought to influence the observational learning: attentional, retentional, behavioral production, and motivational.
Pavlovian conditioning	Pavlovian conditioning, synonymous with classical conditioning is a type of learning found in animals, caused by the association (or pairing) of two stimuli or what Ivan Pavlov described as the learning of conditional behavior, therefore called conditioning.
Confederate	Someone who is posing as a participant in an experiment but is actually assisting the experimenter is a confederate.
Galvanic skin response	Galvanic skin response is a method of measuring the electrical resistance of the skin and interpreting it as an image of activity in certain parts of the body.
Conditional response	A conditional response is elicited by a conditional stimulus in a conditional reflex.

Conditioning	Conditioning describes the process by which behaviors can be learned or modified through interaction with the environment.
Affect	A subjective feeling or emotional tone often accompanied by bodily expressions noticeable to others is called affect.
Stimulus	A change in an environmental condition that elicits a response is a stimulus.
Reinforcement	In operant conditioning, reinforcement is any change in an environment that (a) occurs after the behavior, (b) seems to make that behavior re-occur more often in the future and (c) that reoccurence of behavior must be the result of the change.
Reid	Reid was the founder of the Scottish School of Common Sense, and played an integral role in the Scottish Enlightenment. He advocated direct realism, or common sense realism, and argued strongly against the Theory of Ideas advocated by John Locke and René Descartes.
Avoidance learning	Avoidance learning describes how a learner develops a pattern that will allow him/her to avoid an aversive location or situation. Avoidance learning takes place when a map is created which allows the learner not to go to the place where the aversive is.
Moral judgment	Making decisions about which actions are right and which are wrong is a moral judgment.
Punishment	Punishment is the addtion of a stimulus that reduces the frequency of a response, or the removal of a stimulus that results in a reduction of the response.
Hartup	According to Hartup, the single best childhood predictor of adult adaptation is not school grades, and not classroom behavior, but rather, the adequacy with which the child gets along with other children.
Superstitious behavior	"When small amounts of food are repeatedly given, a 'superstitious ritual' may be set up. This is due not only to the fact that a reinforcing stimulus strengthens any behavior it may happen to follow, even though a contingency has not been explicitly arranged, but also to the fact that the change in behavior resulting from one accidental contingency makes similar accidents more probable."-- Skinner on superstitious behavior.
Verbal Behavior	Verbal Behavior is a book written by B.F. Skinner in which the author presents his ideas on language. For Skinner, speech, along with other forms of communication, was simply a behavior. Skinner argued that each act of speech is an inevitable consequence of the speaker's current environment and his behavioral and sensory history.
Adaptation	Adaptation is a lowering of sensitivity to a stimulus following prolonged exposure to that stimulus. Behavioral adaptations are special ways a particular organism behaves to survive in its natural habitat.
Attention	Attention is the cognitive process of selectively concentrating on one thing while ignoring other things. Psychologists have labeled three types of attention: sustained attention, selective attention, and divided attention.
Operant behavior	Operant behavior is simply emitted by an organism, that is, all organisms are inherently active, emitting responses that operate in the environment. Unlike respondent behavior, which is dependent on the stimulus that preceded it, operant behavior is a function of its consequences.
Generalized imitation	The tendency to imitate modeled behavior even though the imitative behavior is not reinforced is referred to as generalized imitation.
Variable	A variable refers to a measurable factor, characteristic, or attribute of an individual or a system.
Extrasensory perception	Extrasensory perception refers to gaining awareness of or information about objects, events, or another's thoughts through some means other than the known sensory channels.

Go to **Cram101.com** for the Practice Tests for this Chapter.

Fisher	Fisher was a eugenicist, evolutionary biologist, geneticist and statistician. He has been described as "The greatest of Darwin's successors", and a genius who almost single-handedly created the foundations for modern statistical science inventing the techniques of maximum likelihood and analysis of variance.
Human nature	Human nature is the fundamental nature and substance of humans, as well as the range of human behavior that is believed to be invariant over long periods of time and across very different cultural contexts.
Suicide	Suicide behavior is rare in childhood but escalates in adolescence. The suicide rate increases in a linear fashion from adolescence through late adulthood.
Goethe	Goethe argued that laws could not be created by pure rationalism, since geography and history shaped habits and patterns. This stood in sharp contrast to the prevailing Enlightenment view that reason was sufficient to create well-ordered societies and good laws.
Independent variable	A condition in a scientific study that is manipulated (assigned different values by a researcher) so that the effects of the manipulation may be observed is called an independent variable.
Social cognitive theory	Social cognitive theory defines human behavior as a triadic, dynamic, and reciprocal interaction of personal factors, behavior, and the environment. Response consequences of a behavior are used to form expectations of behavioral outcomes. It is the ability to form these expectations that give humans the capability to predict the outcomes of their behavior, before the behavior is performed.
Reinforcement Theory	Reinforcement theory holds that reinforcers can control behavior. The definition has two main components: Contingency, where the occurrence of the reinforcer depends on the occurrence of the learner's response, and Rate of Responding, where the reinforcer serves to increase the learner's rate of responding.
Neal Miller	Neal Miller introduced the concepts of the approach gradient and avoidance gradient. Whether organisms drive toward or away from a positive stimulus or a negative stimulus is a function of the distance that it is from that stimulus.
Theories	Theories are logically self-consistent models or frameworks describing the behavior of a certain natural or social phenomenon. They are broad explanations and predictions concerning phenomena of interest.
Attentional processes	In Bandura's theory of vicarious learning, any activity by an observer that aids in the observation of relevant aspects of a model's behavior and its consequences is referred to as attentional processes.
Retentional processes	Effectiveness of observational learning depends in part on retentional processes. To retain what has been attended to, individuals must somehow encode the information into long-term memory. According to Bandura, humans store the behaviors they observe in the form of mental images or verbal descriptions.
Acquisition	Acquisition is the process of adapting to the environment, learning or becoming conditioned. In classical conditoning terms, it is the initial learning of the stimulus response link, which involves a neutral stimulus being associated with a unconditioned stimulus and becoming a conditioned stimulus.
Motor reproductive processes	In Bandura's theory of vicarious learning, the motor reproductive processes refer to the skills required to perform modeled behavior.
Motivational processes	In observational learning, the motivational processes are the degree to which a behavior is seen to result in a valued outcome (expectancies) will influence the likelihood that one will

adopt a modeled behavior .

Miller and Dollard	Miller and Dollard extended Hull's theory into human social learning conditions. The Social Learning Theory was officially launched in 1941 with their publication of Social Learning and Imitation. It incorporated the principles of Hullian learning: reinforcement, punishment, extinction, and imitation of models.
Skinner	Skinner conducted research on shaping behavior through positive and negative reinforcement, and demonstrated operant conditioning, a technique which he developed in contrast with classical conditioning.
Species	Species refers to a reproductively isolated breeding population.
Innate	Innate behavior is not learned or influenced by the environment, rather, it is present or predisposed at birth.
Longitudinal study	Longitudinal study is a type of developmental study in which the same group of participants is followed and measured for an extended period of time, often years.
Bobo doll	The Bobo doll experiment was conducted by Bandura to study aggressive patterns of behavior. One of the experiment's conclusions was that people can learn through vicarious reinforcement.
Phobia	A persistent, irrational fear of an object, situation, or activity that the person feels compelled to avoid is referred to as a phobia.
Mary Cover Jones	Mary Cover Jones stands out as a pioneer of behavior therapy. Her study of unconditioning a fear of rabbits in a three-year-old named Peter is her most often cited work.
Fear response	In the Mowrer-Miller theory, a response to a threatening or noxious situation that is covert but that is assumed to function as a stimulus to produce measurable physiological changes in the body and observable overt behavior is referred to as the fear response.
Behavior rehearsal	A behavior therapy technique in which a client practices new behavior in the consulting room, often aided by demonstrations and role-play by the therapist is referred to as behavior rehearsal.
Control group	A group that does not receive the treatment effect in an experiment is referred to as the control group or sometimes as the comparison group.
Extinction	In operant extinction, if no reinforcement is delivered after the response, gradually the behavior will no longer occur in the presence of the stimulus. The process is more rapid following continuous reinforcement rather than after partial reinforcement. In Classical Conditioning, repeated presentations of the CS without being followed by the US results in the extinction of the CS.
Median	The median is a number that separates the higher half of a sample, a population, or a probability distribution from the lower half. It is the middle value in a distribution, above and below which lie an equal number of values.
Stages	Stages represent relatively discrete periods of time in which functioning is qualitatively different from functioning at other periods.
Participant modeling	A behavior therapy in which an appropriate response is modeled in graduated steps and the client attempts each step, encouraged and supported by the therapist is participant modeling.
Countercondi-ioning	The process of eliminating a classically conditioned response by pairing the CS with an unconditioned stimulus for a response that is stronger than the conditioned response and that cannot occur at the same time as the CR is called counterconditioning.
Stroke	A stroke occurs when the blood supply to a part of the brain is suddenly interrupted by

	occlusion, by hemorrhage, or other causes
Shaping	The concept of reinforcing successive, increasingly accurate approximations to a target behavior is called shaping. The target behavior is broken down into a hierarchy of elemental steps, each step more sophisticated then the last. By successively reinforcing each of the the elemental steps, a form of differential reinforcement, until that step is learned while extinguishing the step below, the target behavior is gradually achieved.
Vicarious reinforcement	A behavior response that increases as a result of observing other people's behaviors being reinforced is referred to as vicarious reinforcement.
Imitative learning	Imitative learning occurs when the learner internalizes something of a model's behavioral strategies. In Tomasello's theory of cultural learning, imitative learning is the first stage of cultural learning.
Social psychology	Social psychology is the study of the nature and causes of human social behavior, with an emphasis on how people think towards each other and how they relate to each other.
Social learning	Social learning is learning that occurs as a function of observing, retaining and replicating behavior observed in others. Although social learning can occur at any stage in life, it is thought to be particularly important during childhood, particularly as authority becomes important.
Personality	Personality refers to the pattern of enduring characteristics that differentiates a person, the patterns of behaviors that make each individual unique.
Behavior therapy	Behavior therapy refers to the systematic application of the principles of learning to direct modification of a client's problem behaviors.

Go to **Cram101.com** for the Practice Tests for this Chapter.

Learning	Learning is a relatively permanent change in behavior that results from experience. Thus, to attribute a behavioral change to learning, the change must be relatively permanent and must result from experience.
Generalization	In conditioning, the tendency for a conditioned response to be evoked by stimuli that are similar to the stimulus to which the response was conditioned is a generalization. The greater the similarity among the stimuli, the greater the probability of generalization.
Pavlovian conditioning	Pavlovian conditioning, synonymous with classical conditioning is a type of learning found in animals, caused by the association (or pairing) of two stimuli or what Ivan Pavlov described as the learning of conditional behavior, therefore called conditioning.
Conditional response	A conditional response is elicited by a conditional stimulus in a conditional reflex.
Operant learning	A simple form of learning in which an organism learns to engage in behavior because it is reinforced is referred to as operant learning. The consequences of a behavior produce changes in the probability of the behavior's occurence.
Puzzle Box	The puzzle box experiments were motivated in part by Thorndike's dislike for statements that animals made use of extraordinary factulties such as insight in their problem solving. He reasoned that if the animals were showing insight, then their time to escape would suddenly drop to a negligible period, which would also be shown in the learning curve as an abrupt drop; while animals using a more ordinary method of trial and error would show gradual curves. His finding was that cats consistently showed gradual learning. He asserted that the connection between the box and the motions the cat used to escape was strengthened by each escape.
Thorndike	Thorndike worked in animal behavior and the learning process leading to the theory of connectionism. Among his most famous contributions were his research on cats escaping from puzzle boxes, and his formulation of the Law of Effect.
Stimulus generalization	When animals are trained to respond to a single stimulus and test stimuli are introduced that differ from the training stimulus, generally along a single dimension, the systematic decrement in responding typically found has been called the gradient of stimulus generalization.
Stimulus	A change in an environmental condition that elicits a response is a stimulus.
Stimulus control	Linking a particular response with specific stimuli is called stimulus control.
Discrimination	In Learning theory, discrimination refers the ability to distinguish between a conditioned stimulus and other stimuli. It can be brought about by extensive training or differential reinforcement. In social terms, it is the denial of privileges to a person or a group on the basis of prejudice.
Reid	Reid was the founder of the Scottish School of Common Sense, and played an integral role in the Scottish Enlightenment. He advocated direct realism, or common sense realism, and argued strongly against the Theory of Ideas advocated by John Locke and René Descartes.
Carl Hovland	Carl Hovland reported the sleeper effect and collaborated with Irving Janis who would later become famous for his theory of groupthink.
Galvanic skin response	Galvanic skin response is a method of measuring the electrical resistance of the skin and interpreting it as an image of activity in certain parts of the body.
Pitch	Pitch is the psychological interpretation of a sound or musical tone corresponding to its physical frequency
Variable	A variable refers to a measurable factor, characteristic, or attribute of an individual or a

Go to **Cram101.com** for the Practice Tests for this Chapter.

	system.
Semantic generalization	Semantic generalization is the generalization of an abstract property of a stimulus.
Loudness	Loudness is the quality of a sound that is the primary psychological correlate of physical intensity. Loudness is often approximated by a power function with an exponent of 0.6 when plotted vs. sound pressure or 0.3 when plotted vs. sound intensity.
Reinforcement	In operant conditioning, reinforcement is any change in an environment that (a) occurs after the behavior, (b) seems to make that behavior re-occur more often in the future and (c) that reoccurence of behavior must be the result of the change.
Attention	Attention is the cognitive process of selectively concentrating on one thing while ignoring other things. Psychologists have labeled three types of attention: sustained attention, selective attention, and divided attention.
Juvenile delinquent	An adolescent who breaks the law or engages in behavior that is considered illegal is referred to as a juvenile delinquent.
Social skills	Social skills are skills used to interact and communicate with others to assist status in the social structure and other motivations.
Habit	A habit is a response that has become completely separated from its eliciting stimulus. Early learning theorists used the term to describe S-R associations, however not all S-R associations become a habit, rather many are extinguished after reinforcement is withdrawn.
Prejudice	Prejudice in general, implies coming to a judgment on the subject before learning where the preponderance of the evidence actually lies, or formation of a judgement without direct experience.
Emotion	An emotion is a mental states that arise spontaneously, rather than through conscious effort. They are often accompanied by physiological changes.
Punishment	Punishment is the addtion of a stimulus that reduces the frequency of a response, or the removal of a stimulus that results in a reduction of the response.
Extinction	In operant extinction, if no reinforcement is delivered after the response, gradually the behavior will no longer occur in the presence of the stimulus. The process is more rapid following continuous reinforcement rather than after partial reinforcement. In Classical Conditioning, repeated presentations of the CS without being followed by the US results in the extinction of the CS.
Suppression	Suppression is the defense mechanism where a memory is deliberately forgotten.
Discrimination training	Teaching an organism to show a response in the presence of only one of a series of similar stimuli is discrimination training. It is accomplished by alternating the stimuli and reinforcing only the target stimulus.
Evolution	Commonly used to refer to gradual change, evolution is the change in the frequency of alleles within a population from one generation to the next. This change may be caused by different mechanisms, including natural selection, genetic drift, or changes in population (gene flow).
Pavlov	Pavlov first described the phenomenon now known as classical conditioning in experiments with dogs.
Discriminative stimulus	In operant conditioning, a stimulus that indicates that reinforcement is available upon the apporpriate response, is called the discriminative stimulus.
Reinforcer	In operant conditioning, a reinforcer is any stimulus that increases the probability that a preceding behavior will occur again. In Classical Conditioning, the unconditioned stimulus

Go to **Cram101.com** for the Practice Tests for this Chapter.

	(US) is the reinforcer.
Reinforcement value	The reinforcement value is the strength of the rate of responding or the intensity of the response.
Society	The social sciences use the term society to mean a group of people that form a semi-closed (or semi-open) social system, in which most interactions are with other individuals belonging to the group.
Psychiatrist	A psychiatrist is a physician who specializes in the diagnosis and treatment of psychological disorders.
Lashley	Lashley failed to find a single biological locus of memory suggesting to him that memories were not localized to one part of the brain, but were widely distributed throughout the cortex.
Matching to sample	Matching to sample, a discrimination training procedure, is a task where the subject is to select from two or more comparison stimuli the one that matches a sample.
Rate of learning	The rate of learning is the change in responding due to the presence of a stimulus, over time.
Differential outcomes effect	The differential outcomes effect is the finding that discrimination training proceeds more rapidly when different behaviors produce different reinforcers.
Control group	A group that does not receive the treatment effect in an experiment is referred to as the control group or sometimes as the comparison group.
Affect	A subjective feeling or emotional tone often accompanied by bodily expressions noticeable to others is called affect.
Adaptation	Adaptation is a lowering of sensitivity to a stimulus following prolonged exposure to that stimulus. Behavioral adaptations are special ways a particular organism behaves to survive in its natural habitat.
Theories	Theories are logically self-consistent models or frameworks describing the behavior of a certain natural or social phenomenon. They are broad explanations and predictions concerning phenomena of interest.
Spence	Spence attributed improvement in performance to motivational factors rather than habit factors. His Discrimination Learning Theory argued that reinforcement combined with frustration or inhibitors facilitates finding a correct stimulus among a cluster which includes incorrect ones.
Brain	The brain controls and coordinates most movement, behavior and homeostatic body functions such as heartbeat, blood pressure, fluid balance and body temperature. Functions of the brain are responsible for cognition, emotion, memory, motor learning and other sorts of learning. The brain is primarily made up of two types of cells: glia and neurons.
Physiology	The study of the functions and activities of living cells, tissues, and organs and of the physical and chemical phenomena involved is referred to as physiology.
Conditioning	Conditioning describes the process by which behaviors can be learned or modified through interaction with the environment.
Excitatory gradient	In Spence's theory of generalization and discrimination, an excitatory gradient shows an increased tendency to respond to the stimulus or conditioned stimulus as well as to stimuli similar to them.
Inhibitory gradient	In Spence's theory of generalization and discrimination, a gradient showing a decreased tendency to respond to the stimulus or conditioned stimulus and stimuli resembling them is an

Go to **Cram101.com** for the Practice Tests for this Chapter.

inhibitory gradient.

Peak shift	The tendency following discrimination training for the peak of responding in a generalization gradient to shift away from the CS- or S- is called the peak shift.
Hypothesis	A specific statement about behavior or mental processes that is testable through research is a hypothesis.
Deprivation	Deprivation, is the loss or withholding of normal stimulation, nutrition, comfort, love, and so forth; a condition of lacking. The level of stimulation is less than what is required.
Basic research	Basic research has as its primary objective the advancement of knowledge and the theoretical understanding of the relations among variables . It is exploratory and often driven by the researcher's curiosity, interest or hunch.
Insight	Insight refers to a sudden awareness of the relationships among various elements that had previously appeared to be independent of one another.
Concept formation	Concept formation refers to the process of classifying information into meaningful categories based on like or unlike properties.
Herrnstein	Herrnstein was a prominent researcher in comparative psychology who did pioneering work on pigeon intelligence employing the Experimental Analysis of Behavior and formulated the "Matching Law" in the 1960s, a breakthrough in understanding how reinforcement and behavior are linked.
Reasoning	Reasoning is the act of using reason to derive a conclusion from certain premises. There are two main methods to reach a conclusion,deductive reasoning and inductive reasoning.
Relational concept	A concept defined by the relationship between features of an object or between an object and its surroundings is a relational concept.
Kohler	Kohler applied Gestalt principles to study chimpanzees and recorded their ability to devise and use tools and solve problems. In 1917, he published and gained fame with The Mentality of Apes, in which he argued that his subjects, like humans, were capable of insight learning. His work led to a radical revision of learning theory.
Transposition	When a principle learned in one problem-solving situation is applied to the solution of another problem, the process is referred to as transposition.
Mental rotation	The ability to change the position of an image in mental space is called mental rotation.
Reaction time	The amount of time required to respond to a stimulus is referred to as reaction time.
Feedback	Feedback refers to information returned to a person about the effects a response has had.
Subjective experience	Subjective experience refers to reality as it is perceived and interpreted, not as it exists objectively.
Nicotine	Nicotine is an organic compound, an alkaloid found naturally throughout the tobacco plant, with a high concentration in the leaves. It is a potent nerve poison and is included in many insecticides. In lower concentrations, the substance is a stimulant and is one of the main factors leading to the pleasure and habit-forming qualities of tobacco smoking.
Opioid	An opioid is any agent that binds to opioid receptors, found principally in the central nervous system and gastrointestinal tract.
Experimental neurosis	Any bizarre or neurotic-like behavior induced through an experimental procedure such as discrimination training is called experimental neurosis.
Nervous breakdown	Nervous breakdown is often used by laymen to describe a sudden and acute attack of mental illness—for instance, clinical depression or anxiety disorder—in a previously outwardly

Go to **Cram101.com** for the Practice Tests for this Chapter.

healthy person. Breakdowns are the result of chronic and unrelenting nervous strain, and not a sign of weakness.

Harlow	Harlow and his famous wire and cloth surrogate mother monkey studies demonstrated that the need for affection created a stronger bond between mother and infant than did physical needs. He also found that the more discrimination problems the monkeys solved, the better they became at solving them.
Skinner	Skinner conducted research on shaping behavior through positive and negative reinforcement, and demonstrated operant conditioning, a technique which he developed in contrast with classical conditioning.
Paradigm	Paradigm refers to the set of practices that defines a scientific discipline during a particular period of time. It provides a framework from which to conduct research, it ensures that a certain range of phenomena, those on which the paradigm focuses, are explored thoroughly. Itmay also blind scientists to other, perhaps more fruitful, ways of dealing with their subject matter.
Experimental psychology	Experimental psychology is an approach to psychology that treats it as one of the natural sciences, and therefore assumes that it is susceptible to the experimental method.
Innate	Innate behavior is not learned or influenced by the environment, rather, it is present or predisposed at birth.
Secondary Reinforcer	A conditioned reinforcer, sometimes called a secondary reinforcer, is a stimulus or situation that has acquired reinforcing power after being paired in the environment with an unconditioned reinforcer or an earlier conditioned reinforcer.

Learning	Learning is a relatively permanent change in behavior that results from experience. Thus, to attribute a behavioral change to learning, the change must be relatively permanent and must result from experience.
Reinforcement contingencies	The circumstances or rules that determine whether responses lead to the presentation of reinforcers are referred to as reinforcement contingencies. Skinner defined culture as a set of reinforcement contingencies.
Acquisition	Acquisition is the process of adapting to the environment, learning or becoming conditioned. In classical conditoning terms, it is the initial learning of the stimulus response link, which involves a neutral stimulus being associated with a unconditioned stimulus and becoming a conditioned stimulus.
Reinforcement	In operant conditioning, reinforcement is any change in an environment that (a) occurs after the behavior, (b) seems to make that behavior re-occur more often in the future and (c) that reoccurence of behavior must be the result of the change.
Punishment	Punishment is the addtion of a stimulus that reduces the frequency of a response, or the removal of a stimulus that results in a reduction of the response.
Schedule of reinforcement	A schedule of reinforcement is either continuous (the behavior is reinforced each time it occurs) or intermittent (the behavior is reinforced only on certain occasions).
Continuous reinforcement	In continuous reinforcement, every response results in reinforcement.
Extinction	In operant extinction, if no reinforcement is delivered after the response, gradually the behavior will no longer occur in the presence of the stimulus. The process is more rapid following continuous reinforcement rather than after partial reinforcement. In Classical Conditioning, repeated presentations of the CS without being followed by the US results in the extinction of the CS.
Behavior chain	A series of related behaviors, the last of which is followed by reinforcement is a behavior chain.
Skinner	Skinner conducted research on shaping behavior through positive and negative reinforcement, and demonstrated operant conditioning, a technique which he developed in contrast with classical conditioning.
Ratio schedules	Ratio schedules produce higher rates of responding than interval schedules.
Shaping	The concept of reinforcing successive, increasingly accurate approximations to a target behavior is called shaping. The target behavior is broken down into a hierarchy of elemental steps, each step more sophisticated then the last. By successively reinforcing each of the the elemental steps, a form of differential reinforcement, until that step is learned while extinguishing the step below, the target behavior is gradually achieved.
Schedules of Reinforcement	Different combinations of frequency and timing of reinforcement following a behavior are referred to as schedules of reinforcement. They are either continuous (the behavior is reinforced each time it occurs) or intermittent (the behavior is reinforced only on certain occasions).
Reinforcer	In operant conditioning, a reinforcer is any stimulus that increases the probability that a preceding behavior will occur again. In Classical Conditioning, the unconditioned stimulus (US) is the reinforcer.
Post-reinforcement pause	The post-reinforcement pause is a momentary cessation in responding following reinforcement. The phenomenon is primarily associated with fixed interval and fixed ratio schedules.

Go to **Cram101.com** for the Practice Tests for this Chapter.

Variable	A variable refers to a measurable factor, characteristic, or attribute of an individual or a system.
Run rate	The rate at which a behavior occurs once it has resumed following reinforcement is called the run rate.
Affect	A subjective feeling or emotional tone often accompanied by bodily expressions noticeable to others is called affect.
Variable ratio	In a variable ratio schedule of reinforcement, the number of responses required between reinforcements varies, but on average equals a predetermined number. The variable ratio schedule produces both the highest rate of responding and the greatest resistance to extinction.
Society	The social sciences use the term society to mean a group of people that form a semi-closed (or semi-open) social system, in which most interactions are with other individuals belonging to the group.
Fixed interval	In a fixed interval schedule of reinforcement, reinforcement occurs after the passage of a specified length of time from the beginning of training or from the last reinforcement, provided that at least one response occurred in that time period.
Species	Species refers to a reproductively isolated breeding population.
Variable interval	In a variable interval schedule of reinforcement, reinforcement occurs after the passage of a varying length of time around an average, provided that at least one response occurred in that period.
Variable duration	Variable duration schedule is a reinforcement schedule in which reinforcement is contingent on the continuous performance of a behavior for a period of time, with the length of the time varying around an average.
Premack principle	That any high-frequency response can be used to reinforce a low-frequency response is called the Premack Principle.
Differential reinforcement	Any training procedure in which certain kinds of behavior are systematically reinforced and others are not is called differential reinforcement. Differential reinforcement involves both reinforcement and extinction.
Noncontingent reinforcement	Noncontingent reinforcement refers to the procedure of providing reinforcers independently of behavior.
Fixed time	In a fixed time schedule of reinforcement, reinforcement is delivered independently of behavior at fixed time intervals.
Compensation	In personaility, compensation, according to Adler, is an effort to overcome imagined or real inferiorities by developing one's abilities.
Superstitious behavior	"When small amounts of food are repeatedly given, a 'superstitious ritual' may be set up. This is due not only to the fact that a reinforcing stimulus strengthens any behavior it may happen to follow, even though a contingency has not been explicitly arranged, but also to the fact that the change in behavior resulting from one accidental contingency makes similar accidents more probable."-- Skinner on superstitious behavior.
Stretching the ratio	The procedure of gradually increasing the number of responses required for reinforcement is called stretching the ratio.
Stages	Stages represent relatively discrete periods of time in which functioning is qualitatively different from functioning at other periods.
Ratio strain	A ratio strain is the disruption of the pattern of responding due to stretching the ratio of

Go to **Cram101.com** for the Practice Tests for this Chapter.

reinforcement too abruptly or too far.

Intermittent reinforcement	In an intermittent reinforcement schedule, a designated response is reinforced only some of the time.
Resistance to extinction	Resistance to extinction is the phenomenon that occurs when an organism continues to make a response even after the delivery of the reinforcer for the response has been all or partially eliminated.
Law of effect	The law of effect is a principle of psychology described by Edward Thorndike in 1898. It holds that responses to stimuli that produce a satisfying or pleasant effect in a particular situation are more likely to occur again in the situation. Conversely, responses that produce a discomforting or unpleasant effect are less likely to occur again in the situation
Paradoxical	Paradoxical intention refers to instructing clients to do the opposite of the desired behavior. Telling an impotent man not to have sex or an insomniac not to sleep reduces anxiety to perform.
Discrimination	In Learning theory, discrimination refers the ability to distinguish between a conditioned stimulus and other stimuli. It can be brought about by extensive training or differential reinforcement. In social terms, it is the denial of privileges to a person or a group on the basis of prejudice.
Hypothesis	A specific statement about behavior or mental processes that is testable through research is a hypothesis.
Theories	Theories are logically self-consistent models or frameworks describing the behavior of a certain natural or social phenomenon. They are broad explanations and predictions concerning phenomena of interest.
Depression	In everyday language depression refers to any downturn in mood, which may be relatively transitory and perhaps due to something trivial. This is differentiated from Clinical depression which is marked by symptoms that last two weeks or more and are so severe that they interfere with daily living.
Illusion	An illusion is a distortion of a sensory perception.
Multiple schedule	A complex reinforcement schedule in which two or more simple schedules alternate, with each schedule associated with a particular stimulus is the multiple schedule.
Stimulus	A change in an environmental condition that elicits a response is a stimulus.
Mixed schedule	A mixed schedule is a complex reinforcement schedule in which two or more simple schedules alternate.
Chain schedule	A complex reinforcement schedule that consists of a series of simple schedules, each of which is associated with a particular stimulus, with reinforcement delivered only on completion of the last schedule in the series is a chain schedule of reinforcement.
Tandem schedule	A tandem schedule is a complex reinforcement schedule that consists of a series of simple schedules, with reinforcement delivered only on completion of the last schedule in the series.
Cooperative schedule	A complex reinforcement schedule in which reinforcement is contingent on the behavior of two or more individuals is referred to as the cooperative schedule.
Concurrent schedule	A concurrent schedule is a complex reinforcement schedule in which two or more simple schedules are available at the same time.
Matching law	The Matching Law describes the fact that, under concurrent schedules of reinforcement, an organisms' relative rate of responding to each alternative tends to match each alternative's

relative rate of reinforcement.

Herrnstein	Herrnstein was a prominent researcher in comparative psychology who did pioneering work on pigeon intelligence employing the Experimental Analysis of Behavior and formulated the "Matching Law" in the 1960s, a breakthrough in understanding how reinforcement and behavior are linked.
Insight	Insight refers to a sudden awareness of the relationships among various elements that had previously appeared to be independent of one another.
Gene	A gene is an ultramicroscopic area of the chromosome. It is the smallest physical unit of the DNA molecule that carries a piece of hereditary information.
Psychoactive drug	A psychoactive drug or psychotropic substance is a chemical that alters brain function, resulting in temporary changes in perception, mood, consciousness, or behavior. Such drugs are often used for recreational and spiritual purposes, as well as in medicine, especially for treating neurological and psychological illnesses.
Population	Population refers to all members of a well-defined group of organisms, events, or things.
Malingering	Malingering is a medical and psychological term that refers to an individual faking the symptoms of mental or physical disorders for a myriad of reasons such as fraud, dereliction of responsibilities, attempting to obtain medications or to lighten criminal sentences.
Operant behavior	Operant behavior is simply emitted by an organism, that is, all organisms are inherently active, emitting responses that operate in the environment. Unlike respondent behavior, which is dependent on the stimulus that preceded it, operant behavior is a function of its consequences.
Chronic	Chronic refers to a relatively long duration, usually more than a few months.
Baseline period	In a within-subject experiment, a period of observation during which no attempt is made to modify the behavior under study is referred to as the baseline period.
Construct	A generalized concept, such as anxiety or gravity, is a construct.
Personality	Personality refers to the pattern of enduring characteristics that differentiates a person, the patterns of behaviors that make each individual unique.
Motivation	In psychology, motivation is the driving force (desire) behind all actions of an organism.
Cocaine	Cocaine is a crystalline tropane alkaloid that is obtained from the leaves of the coca plant. It is a stimulant of the central nervous system and an appetite suppressant, creating what has been described as a euphoric sense of happiness and increased energy.
Deprivation	Deprivation, is the loss or withholding of normal stimulation, nutrition, comfort, love, and so forth; a condition of lacking. The level of stimulation is less than what is required.
Baseline	Measure of a particular behavior or process taken before the introduction of the independent variable or treatment is called the baseline.
Brain	The brain controls and coordinates most movement, behavior and homeostatic body functions such as heartbeat, blood pressure, fluid balance and body temperature. Functions of the brain are responsible for cognition, emotion, memory, motor learning and other sorts of learning. The brain is primarily made up of two types of cells: glia and neurons.
Positive reinforcer	In operant conditioning, a stimulus that is presented after a response that increases the likelihood that the response will be repeated is a positive reinforcer.
Variable time schedule	Variable time schedule is a reinforcement schedule in which reinforcement is delivered at varying intervals regardless of what the organism does.

Go to **Cram101.com** for the Practice Tests for this Chapter.

Metaphor	A metaphor is a rhetorical trope where a comparison is made between two seemingly unrelated subjects
Plato	According to Plato, people must come equipped with most of their knowledge and need only hints and contemplation to complete it. Plato suggested that the brain is the mechanism of mental processes and that one gained knowledge by reflecting on the contents of one's mind.
Skinner	Skinner conducted research on shaping behavior through positive and negative reinforcement, and demonstrated operant conditioning, a technique which he developed in contrast with classical conditioning.
Natural selection	Natural selection is a process by which biological populations are altered over time, as a result of the propagation of heritable traits that affect the capacity of individual organisms to survive and reproduce.
Learning	Learning is a relatively permanent change in behavior that results from experience. Thus, to attribute a behavioral change to learning, the change must be relatively permanent and must result from experience.
Physiology	The study of the functions and activities of living cells, tissues, and organs and of the physical and chemical phenomena involved is referred to as physiology.
Affect	A subjective feeling or emotional tone often accompanied by bodily expressions noticeable to others is called affect.
Discrimination	In Learning theory, discrimination refers the ability to distinguish between a conditioned stimulus and other stimuli. It can be brought about by extensive training or differential reinforcement. In social terms, it is the denial of privileges to a person or a group on the basis of prejudice.
Cognitive structure	According to Piaget, the number of schemata available to an organism at any given time constitutes that organism's cognitive structure. How the organism interacts with its environment depends on the current cognitive structure available. As the cognitive structure develops, new assimilations can occur.
Retention interval	Retention interval is the time between training and testing in which forgetting may occur.
Free recall	In memory research, a task in which a subject recalls information without specific cues or prompts is referred to as free recall.
Anagram	An anagram is a type of word play, the result of rearranging the letters of a word or phrase to produce other words, using all the original letters exactly once.
Relearning	Relearning refers to a measure of retention used in experiments on memory. Material is usually relearned more quickly than it is learned initially.
Ebbinghaus	Ebbinghaus pioneered the development of experimental methods for the measurement of rote learning and memory.
Permanent memory	Hebb did not believe that any chemical process could occur fast enough to accomodate immediate memory yet remain stable enough to accomodate permanent memory. Thus the notion of two memory systems was proposed: long-term memory (LTM), and short-term memory (STM).
Consciousness	The awareness of the sensations, thoughts, and feelings being experienced at a given moment is called consciousness.
Loftus	Loftus works on human memory and how it can be changed by facts, ideas, suggestions and other forms of post-event information. One of her famous studies include the "car accident" study, which was an example of the misinformation effect.

Go to **Cram101.com** for the Practice Tests for this Chapter.

Brain	The brain controls and coordinates most movement, behavior and homeostatic body functions such as heartbeat, blood pressure, fluid balance and body temperature. Functions of the brain are responsible for cognition, emotion, memory, motor learning and other sorts of learning. The brain is primarily made up of two types of cells: glia and neurons.
Sigmund Freud	Sigmund Freud was the founder of the psychoanalytic school, based on his theory that unconscious motives control much behavior, that particular kinds of unconscious thoughts and memories are the source of neurosis, and that neurosis could be treated through bringing these unconscious thoughts and memories to consciousness in psychoanalytic treatment.
Penfield	Penfield treated patients with severe epilepsy by destroying nerve cells in the brain. Before operating, he stimulated the brain with electrical probes while the patients were conscious on the operating table, and observed their responses. It allowed him to create maps of sensory and motor functions.
Anxiety	Anxiety is a complex combination of the feeling of fear, apprehension and worry often accompanied by physical sensations such as palpitations, chest pain and/or shortness of breath.
Case study	A carefully drawn biography that may be obtained through interviews, questionnaires, and psychological tests is called a case study.
Epilepsy	Epilepsy is a chronic neurological condition characterized by recurrent unprovoked neural discharges. It is commonly controlled with medication, although surgical methods are used as well.
Seizure	A seizure is a temporary alteration in brain function expressed as a changed mental state, tonic or clonic movements and various other symptoms. They are due to temporary abnormal electrical activity of a group of brain cells.
Sensation	Sensation is the first stage in the chain of biochemical and neurologic events that begins with the impinging of a stimulus upon the receptor cells of a sensory organ, which then leads to perception, the mental state that is reflected in statements like "I see a uniformly blue wall."
Delayed matching to sample	Delayed matching to sample is an experimental method of measuring forgetting in which the opportunity to match a sample follows a retention interval.
Matching to sample	Matching to sample, a discrimination training procedure, is a task where the subject is to select from two or more comparison stimuli the one that matches a sample.
Stimulus	A change in an environmental condition that elicits a response is a stimulus.
Variable	A variable refers to a measurable factor, characteristic, or attribute of an individual or a system.
Extinction method	A method of measuring forgetting by comparing the rate of extinction after a retention interval with the rate of extinction immediately after training is the extinction method.
Extinction	In operant extinction, if no reinforcement is delivered after the response, gradually the behavior will no longer occur in the presence of the stimulus. The process is more rapid following continuous reinforcement rather than after partial reinforcement. In Classical Conditioning, repeated presentations of the CS without being followed by the US results in the extinction of the CS.
Gradient degradation	Gradient degradation is a method of measuring forgetting in which a behavior is tested for generalization before and after a retention interval. A flattening of the generalization gradient indicates forgetting.

Go to **Cram101.com** for the Practice Tests for this Chapter.

Generalization	In conditioning, the tendency for a conditioned response to be evoked by stimuli that are similar to the stimulus to which the response was conditioned is a generalization. The greater the similarity among the stimuli, the greater the probability of generalization.
Stimulus control	Linking a particular response with specific stimuli is called stimulus control.
Gagne	Gagne stipulates that there are several different types or levels of learning. The significance of these classifications is that different types of learning require different types of instruction. He identified five major categories of learning: verbal information; intellectual skills; cognitive strategies; motor skills; and, attitudes. Gagne suggests that learning tasks for intellectual skills can be organized in a hierarchy according to complexity.
Nonsense syllable	A nonsense syllable is a consonant-vowel-consonant combination that does not spell a word. It is an experimental methodology invented by Ebbinghaus to control for the meaningfulness of the material in studies of memory.
Reinforcement	In operant conditioning, reinforcement is any change in an environment that (a) occurs after the behavior, (b) seems to make that behavior re-occur more often in the future and (c) that reoccurence of behavior must be the result of the change.
Attention	Attention is the cognitive process of selectively concentrating on one thing while ignoring other things. Psychologists have labeled three types of attention: sustained attention, selective attention, and divided attention.
Overlearning	Continued rehearsal of material after one first appears to have mastered it is called overlearning.
Herbert Simon	Herbert Simon was a pioneer in the field of artificial intelligence, creating with Allen Newell the Logic Theory Machine (1956) and the General Problem Solver (GPS) (1957) programs. GPS was possibly the first method of separating problem solving strategy from information about particular problems.
Hypothesis	A specific statement about behavior or mental processes that is testable through research is a hypothesis.
Proactive interference	Proactive interference occurs when information learned earlier disrupts the recall of material learned later. This can become a problem when new information cannot be used correctly as it is interfered with by the older information.
Social psychologists	Social psychologists study the nature and causes of human social behavior, emphasizing on how people think and relate towards each other.
Retroactive interference	Retroactive interference occurs when the material learned later disrupts retrieval of information learned earlier, so old information overlaps with new information.
Paired associate	Paired associate is a method where subjects learn pairs of items so that when they are shown one member of the pair, they can respond with the other.
Retroactive inhibition	Retroactive inhibition refers to a situation where learning one thing inhibits the retention of something that was learned earlier.
Cue-dependent forgetting	Cue-dependent forgetting is a failure to recall a memory due to missing associated stimuli or cues.
Hormone	A hormone is a chemical messenger from one cell (or group of cells) to another. The best known are those produced by endocrine glands, but they are produced by nearly every organ system. The function of hormones is to serve as a signal to the target cells; the action of the hormone is determined by the pattern of secretion and the signal transduction of the receiving tissue.

Go to **Cram101.com** for the Practice Tests for this Chapter.

Baddeley	Baddeley introduced a multicomponent model of working memory for the temporary maintenance and manipulation of information. It emphasizes the functional importance of such a system rather than its use as the unitary short-term store proposed by Atkinson and Shiffrin.
Applied research	Applied research is done to solve specific, practical questions; its primary aim is not to gain knowledge for its own sake. It can be exploratory but often it is descriptive. It is almost always done on the basis of basic research.
Species	Species refers to a reproductively isolated breeding population.
Forgetting curve	Ebbinghaus' forgetting curve illustrates the decline of memory retention in time. A typical graph of the forgetting curve shows that humans tend to halve their memory of newly learned knowledge in a matter of days or weeks unless they consciously review the learned material.
Questionnaire	A self-report method of data collection or clinical assessment method in which the individual being studied checks off items on a printed list, answers multiple-choice questions, or writes out answers to essay questions aimed at producing a selfdescription is called questionnaire.
Hypnosis	Hypnosis is a psychological state whose existence and effects are strongly debated. Some believe that it is a state under which the subject's mind becomes so suggestible that the hypnotist, the one who induces the state, can establish communication with the subconscious mind of the subject and command behavior that the subject would not choose to perform in a conscious state.
Regression	Return to a form of behavior characteristic of an earlier stage of development is called regression.
Plasticity	The capacity for modification and change is referred to as plasticity.
Retrieval	Retrieval is the location of stored information and its subsequent return to consciousness. It is the third stage of information processing.
Mnemonic	A mnemonic is a memory aid. They are often verbal, are sometimes in verse form, and are often used to remember lists.
Mercury	Elemental, liquid mercury is slightly toxic, while its vapor, compounds and salts are highly toxic and have been implicated as causing brain and liver damage when ingested, inhaled or contacted. Because mercury is easily transferred across the placenta, the embryo is highly susceptible to birth defects.
Peg word system	A peg word system is a mnemonic technique for memorizing lists. It works by first memorizing an object for each number from 0 to 99 (or from 0 to 999, etc.). Those objects form the "pegs" of the system. Then in the future, to rapidly memorize a list of arbitrary objects, each one is associated with the appropriate peg.
Method of loci	Method of loci is a mnemonic device that involves taking an imaginary walk along a familiar path where images of items to be remembered are associated with certain locations.
Schopenhauer	For Schopenhauer, human will had ontological primacy over the intellect; in other words, desire is understood to be prior to thought, and, in a parallel sense, will is said to be prior to being.
Neuropsychol-gist	A psychologist concerned with the relationships among cognition, affect, behavior, and brain function is a neuropsychologist.
Social psychology	Social psychology is the study of the nature and causes of human social behavior, with an emphasis on how people think towards each other and how they relate to each other.
Insight	Insight refers to a sudden awareness of the relationships among various elements that had previously appeared to be independent of one another.

Spontaneous recovery	The recurrence of an extinguished response as a function of the passage of time is referred to as spontaneous recovery.

Human nature	Human nature is the fundamental nature and substance of humans, as well as the range of human behavior that is believed to be invariant over long periods of time and across very different cultural contexts.
Learning	Learning is a relatively permanent change in behavior that results from experience. Thus, to attribute a behavioral change to learning, the change must be relatively permanent and must result from experience.
Washoe	Washoe is a chimpanzee who was the first non-human to acquire at least some elements of American Sign Language (ASL), as part of a controversial research experiment into animal intelligence.
Fixed action pattern	A behavior that occurs in essentially identical fashion among most members of a species, that is elicited by a specific environmental stimulus, and is typically more complex than a reflex, is a fixed action pattern.
Lamarck	Lamarck proposed a theory of evolution based on the idea that individuals adapt during their own lifetimes and transmit traits they acquire to their offspring, the "inheritance of acquired traits." In spite of its being largely discredited, Darwin and others acknowledged him as an early proponent of ideas about evolution.
Adaptation	Adaptation is a lowering of sensitivity to a stimulus following prolonged exposure to that stimulus. Behavioral adaptations are special ways a particular organism behaves to survive in its natural habitat.
Natural selection	Natural selection is a process by which biological populations are altered over time, as a result of the propagation of heritable traits that affect the capacity of individual organisms to survive and reproduce.
Evolution	Commonly used to refer to gradual change, evolution is the change in the frequency of alleles within a population from one generation to the next. This change may be caused by different mechanisms, including natural selection, genetic drift, or changes in population (gene flow).
Theories	Theories are logically self-consistent models or frameworks describing the behavior of a certain natural or social phenomenon. They are broad explanations and predictions concerning phenomena of interest.
Darwin	Darwin achieved lasting fame as originator of the theory of evolution through natural selection. His book Expression of Emotions in Man and Animals is generally considered the first text on comparative psychology.
McDougall	McDougall was important in the development of the theory of instinct and of social psychology. Opposing behaviorism, he argued that behavior was generally goal-oriented and purposive, an approach he called hormic psychology; in the theory of motivation he held that individuals are motivated by a significant number of inherited instincts so they might not always understand their own goals.
Hypothesis	A specific statement about behavior or mental processes that is testable through research is a hypothesis.
Social role	Social role refers to expected behavior patterns associated with particular social positions.
Heredity	Heredity is the transfer of characteristics from parent to offspring through their genes.
Anatomy	Anatomy is the branch of biology that deals with the structure and organization of living things. It can be divided into animal anatomy (zootomy) and plant anatomy (phytonomy). Major branches of anatomy include comparative anatomy, histology, and human anatomy.
Variability	Statistically, variability refers to how much the scores in a distribution spread out, away from the mean.

Identical twins	Identical twins occur when a single egg is fertilized to form one zygote (monozygotic) but the zygote then divides into two separate embryos. The two embryos develop into foetuses sharing the same womb. Monozygotic twins are genetically identical unless there has been a mutation in development, and they are almost always the same gender.
Gene	A gene is an ultramicroscopic area of the chromosome. It is the smallest physical unit of the DNA molecule that carries a piece of hereditary information.
Species	Species refers to a reproductively isolated breeding population.
Nervous system	The body's electrochemical communication circuitry, made up of billions of neurons is a nervous system.
Prenatal	Prenatal period refers to the time from conception to birth.
Early childhood	Early childhood refers to the developmental period extending from the end of infancy to about 5 or 6 years of age; sometimes called the preschool years.
Infancy	The developmental period that extends from birth to 18 or 24 months is called infancy.
Nerve	A nerve is an enclosed, cable-like bundle of nerve fibers or axons, which includes the glia that ensheath the axons in myelin. Neurons are sometimes called nerve cells, though this term is technically imprecise since many neurons do not form nerves.
Galton	Galton was one of the first experimental psychologists, and the founder of the field of Differential Psychology, which concerns itself with individual differences rather than on common trends. He created the statistical methods correlation and regression.
John Stuart Mill	John Stuart Mill formulated five methods of induction -- the method of agreement, the method of difference, the joint or double method of agreement and difference, the method of residues, and that of concomitant variations. The common feature of these methods, the one real method of scientific inquiry, is that of elimination
James Mill	With his Analysis of the Mind and his Fragment on Mackintosh , James Mill acquired a position in the history of psychology and ethics. He carried out the principle of association into the analysis of the complex emotional states, as the affections, the aesthetic emotions and the moral sentiment, all which he endeavoured to resolve into pleasurable and painful sensations.
Enrichment	Deliberately making an environment more novel, complex, and perceptually or intellectually stimulating is referred to as enrichment.
Child abuse	Child abuse is the physical or psychological maltreatment of a child.
Anecdotal evidence	Anecdotal evidence is unreliable evidence based on personal experience that has not been empirically tested, and which is often used in an argument as if it had been scientifically or statistically proven. The person using anecdotal evidence may or may not be aware of the fact that, by doing so, they are generalizing.
Brain	The brain controls and coordinates most movement, behavior and homeostatic body functions such as heartbeat, blood pressure, fluid balance and body temperature. Functions of the brain are responsible for cognition, emotion, memory, motor learning and other sorts of learning. The brain is primarily made up of two types of cells: glia and neurons.
Malnutrition	Malnutrition is a general term for the medical condition in a person or animal caused by an unbalanced diet—either too little or too much food, or a diet missing one or more important nutrients.
Trauma	Trauma refers to a severe physical injury or wound to the body caused by an external force, or a psychological shock having a lasting effect on mental life.
Critical period	A period of time when an innate response can be elicited by a particular stimulus is referred

	to as the critical period.
Stages	Stages represent relatively discrete periods of time in which functioning is qualitatively different from functioning at other periods.
Imprinting	Imprinting describes any kind of critical period sensitive learning (learning occurring at a particular age or a particular life stage) that is rapid and apparently independent of the consequences of behavior.
Lorenz	Lorenz demonstrated how incubator-hatched geese would imprint on the first suitable moving stimulus they saw within what he called a "critical period" of about 36 hours shortly after hatching. Most famously, the goslings would imprint on Lorenz himself .
Harlow	Harlow and his famous wire and cloth surrogate mother monkey studies demonstrated that the need for affection created a stronger bond between mother and infant than did physical needs. He also found that the more discrimination problems the monkeys solved, the better they became at solving them.
Surrogate mother	A surrogate mother is a woman who carries a child for a couple or single person with the intention of giving that child up once it is born.
Social skills	Social skills are skills used to interact and communicate with others to assist status in the social structure and other motivations.
Reinforcement	In operant conditioning, reinforcement is any change in an environment that (a) occurs after the behavior, (b) seems to make that behavior re-occur more often in the future and (c) that reoccurence of behavior must be the result of the change.
Preparedness	The species-specific biological predisposition to learn in certain ways is called preparedness.
Sexual orientation	Sexual orientation refers to the sex or gender of people who are the focus of a person's amorous or erotic desires, fantasies, and spontaneous feelings, the gender(s) toward which one is primarily "oriented".
Innate	Innate behavior is not learned or influenced by the environment, rather, it is present or predisposed at birth.
Instinctive Drift	The tendency of animals to revert to innate behavior that interferes with learning is called instinctive drift.
Conditioning	Conditioning describes the process by which behaviors can be learned or modified through interaction with the environment.
Skinner	Skinner conducted research on shaping behavior through positive and negative reinforcement, and demonstrated operant conditioning, a technique which he developed in contrast with classical conditioning.
Continuum of preparedness	A continuum of preparedness is the idea that organisms are genetically disposed to learn some things and not others.
Autoshaping	In autoshaping a light is reliably turned on shortly before pigeons are given food. The pigeons naturally, unconditionally, peck (unconditional response) at the food (unconditional stimulus) given them, but through learning, conditionally, came to peck (conditional response) at the light source (conditional stimulus) that predicts food.
Sign tracking	Sign tracking refers to a procedure in which a stimulus is followed by a reinforcer regardless of what the organism does. The procedure often results in the 'shaping' of behavior without reinforcement.
Pavlovian	Pavlovian conditioning, synonymous with classical conditioning is a type of learning found in

conditioning	animals, caused by the association (or pairing) of two stimuli or what Ivan Pavlov described as the learning of conditional behavior, therefore called conditioning.
Psycholinguist	A specialist in the psychology of language and language development is called a psycholinguist.
Phobia	A persistent, irrational fear of an object, situation, or activity that the person feels compelled to avoid is referred to as a phobia.
Scheme	According to Piaget, a hypothetical mental structure that permits the classification and organization of new information is called a scheme.
Attachment	Attachment is the tendency to seek closeness to another person and feel secure when that person is present.
Wolpe	Wolpe is best known for applying classical conditioning principles to the treatment of phobias, called systematic desensitization. Any "neutral" stimulus, simple or complex that happens to make an impact on an individual at about the time that a fear reaction is evoked acquires the ability to evoke fear subsequently. An acquired CS-CR relationship should be extinguishable.
Latent inhibition	If after the habituation of a stimulus, it is later paired with a US the conditioning may be weak and unstable. This effect is called latent inhibition.
Society	The social sciences use the term society to mean a group of people that form a semi-closed (or semi-open) social system, in which most interactions are with other individuals belonging to the group.
A priori	The term A Priori is considered to mean propositional knowledge that can be had without, or "prior to", experience.
Individual differences	Individual differences psychology studies the ways in which individual people differ in their behavior. This is distinguished from other aspects of psychology in that although psychology is ostensibly a study of individuals, modern psychologists invariably study groups.
Sociobiology	Sociobiology is a synthesis of scientific disciplines that attempts to explain behavior in all species by considering the evolutionary advantages of social behaviors.
Experimental manipulation	The change that an experimenter deliberately produces in a situation under study is called the experimental manipulation.
Aba reversal design	An ABA reversal design is a type of within subject experiment in which behavior is observed before and after an experimental manipulation. The original condition is restored, sometimes followed again by the experimental condition.
Attentional processes	In Bandura's theory of vicarious learning, any activity by an observer that aids in the observation of relevant aspects of a model's behavior and its consequences is referred to as attentional processes.
Vicarious learning	Vicarious learning is learning without specific reinforcement for one's behavior. It is learning by observing others.
Bandura	Bandura is best known for his work on social learning theory or Social Cognitivism. His famous Bobo doll experiment illustrated that people learn from observing others.
Countercondi-ioning	The process of eliminating a classically conditioned response by pairing the CS with an unconditioned stimulus for a response that is stronger than the conditioned response and that cannot occur at the same time as the CR is called counterconditioning.
Aversion therapy	Aversion therapy is a now largely discredited form of treatment in which the patient is exposed to a stimulus while simultaneously being hurt or made ill. The theory is that the

	patient will come to associate the stimulus with unpleasant sensations and will no longer seek it out.
Stimulus	A change in an environmental condition that elicits a response is a stimulus.
Backward chaining	Backward chaining starts with a list of goals and works backwards to see if there is data which will allow it to conclude any of these goals.
Chaining	Chaining involves reinforcing individual responses occurring in a sequence to form a complex behavior. It is frequently used for training behavioral sequences that are beyond the current repetoire of the learner.
Backward conditioning	A classical conditioning procedure in which the unconditioned stimulus is presented before the conditioned stimulus is called backward conditioning. It is seldom effective.
Baseline period	In a within-subject experiment, a period of observation during which no attempt is made to modify the behavior under study is referred to as the baseline period.
Overt behavior	An action or response that is directly observable and measurable is an overt behavior.
Behavior chain	A series of related behaviors, the last of which is followed by reinforcement is a behavior chain.
Independent variable	A condition in a scientific study that is manipulated (assigned different values by a researcher) so that the effects of the manipulation may be observed is called an independent variable.
Compound stimulus	A compound stimulus refers to two or more stimuli presented simultaneously.
Blocking	If the one of the two members of a compound stimulus fails to produce the CR due to an earlier conditioning of the other member of the compound stimulus, blocking has occurred.
Case study	A carefully drawn biography that may be obtained through interviews, questionnaires, and psychological tests is called a case study.
Chain schedule	A complex reinforcement schedule that consists of a series of simple schedules, each of which is associated with a particular stimulus, with reinforcement delivered only on completion of the last schedule in the series is a chain schedule of reinforcement.

Go to **Cram101.com** for the Practice Tests for this Chapter.